23 Ready-To-Go Lesson Pl[...]

SCIENCE

GRADE 2

www.themailbox.com

D1707896

What Are Lifesaver Lessons®?

Lifesaver Lessons® are well-planned, easy-to-implement, curriculum-based lessons. Each lesson contains a complete materials list, step-by-step instructions, a reproducible activity or pattern, and several extension activities.

How Do I Use A Lifesaver Lesson?

Each Lifesaver Lesson is designed to decrease your preparation time and increase the amount of quality teaching time with your students. These lessons are great for introducing or reinforcing new concepts. You may want to look through the lessons to see what types of materials to gather. After completing a lesson, be sure to check out the fun-filled extension activities.

What Materials Will I Need?

Most of the materials for each lesson can be easily found in your classroom or school. Check the list of materials below for any items you may need to gather or purchase.

- crayons
- colored chalk
- scissors
- glue
- writing paper
- construction paper
- duplicating paper
- bulletin-board paper
- chart paper

- tagboard
- stapler
- index cards
- world map
- game markers
- container to hold paper strips
- tape
- school lunch menu
- discarded magazines

- X-acto® knife
- craft sticks
- materials to demonstrate each of the six types of simple machines
- real estate ads (optional)

Project Editors:
Cynthia Holcomb, Sharon Murphy

Writers:
Rebecca Brudwick, Elizabeth Chappell,
Amy Erickson, Cynthia Holcomb, Susie Kapaun, Martha Kelly,
Laura Mihalenko, Sharon Murphy

Artists:
Jennifer Tipton Bennett, Cathy Spangler Bruce,
Nick Greenwood, Rob Mayworth, Kimberly Richard,
Rebecca Saunders, Donna K. Teal

Cover Artist:
Jennifer Tipton Bennett

Lifesaver Lessons®

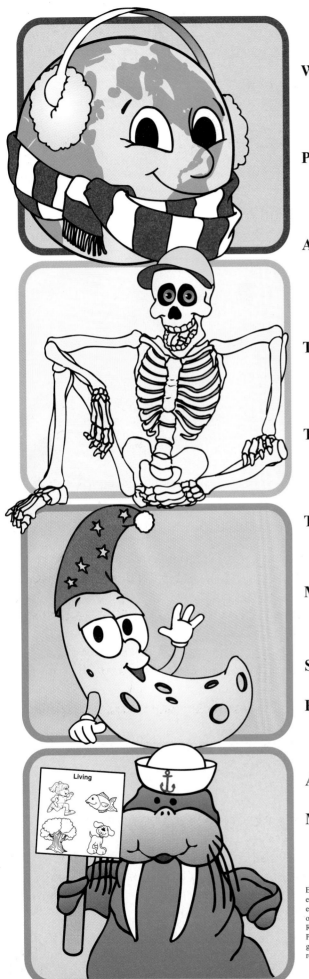

Table Of Contents

Manufactured in the United States
10 9 8 7 6 5 4 3

Oh, The Weather Outside...

Fun is in the forecast with this weather identification activity!

Skill: Identifying types of weather

Estimated Lesson Time: 25 minutes

Teacher Preparation:
Duplicate page 5 for each student.

Materials:
1 copy of page 5 per student
scissors
glue

Background Information:

Weather—the condition of the atmosphere around us—affects everyone in some manner, from wardrobe selections to the growth of crops. Information about several different types of weather is provided below.

- **Sunny:** All of the Earth's energy comes from the Sun. Because the Earth is round, the Sun's rays strike its surface at different angles, resulting in an uneven distribution of heat.
- **Windy:** Some parts of the Earth are warmed more than others, which results in wind—moving air.
- **Cloudy:** Clouds are made of millions of water droplets or ice crystals. They are named for their shape and height.
- **Precipitation:** Precipitation is any form of water that falls from the atmosphere and reaches the ground. Rain and snow are the most common types.
  - **Rain:** When water droplets become so heavy that they fall from clouds, rain is produced.
  - **Snow:** Snow is formed when ice crystals in a cloud cling together.
  - **Sleet:** Sleet is partly melted snow or a mixture of snow and rain.
- **Extreme Weather**
  - **Thunderstorm:** A thunderstorm produces lightning and thunder. Lightning is a huge electric spark. Thunder is the sound of air quickly expanding as lightning heats it.
  - **Tornado:** A tornado is a dangerous and powerful funnel-shaped whirlwind of spinning, rising air.
  - **Hurricane:** A hurricane is a strong, whirling storm that measures 200 to 300 miles in diameter and has winds of 74 miles per hour or more.
  - **Blizzard:** A blizzard is a heavy snowstorm with strong winds and low temperatures.

Introducing The Lesson:

Write the words "windy," "rainy," and "snowy" on the chalkboard. Ask youngsters to determine what these words have in common. Lead students to the conclusion that each word is a type of weather. Challenge students to brainstorm other types of weather as you record their responses on the chalkboard. Then discuss with youngsters how each of these weather conditions affects our lives.

Steps:

1. Use the Background Information on page 3 to define the term *weather* and provide details about several different weather conditions.

2. Explain that weather influences our lives in many respects, including clothing and activity choices. Name a weather condition and invite students to identify clothing and activities that would be appropriate for it. (Be sure to caution students that outside activities are not safe during severe weather.) Continue this discussion in a like manner with other types of weather.

3. Then give each student a copy of page 5. Read the chart with students and review the picture cards at the bottom of the page.

4. Have each youngster cut apart his picture cards. Then have him use the information provided on his chart and glue each card in the correct space.

5. Instruct each student to use information from the discussion to write appropriate facts and activities in the remaining spaces on his sheet.

6. Challenge youngsters to complete the Bonus Box activity.

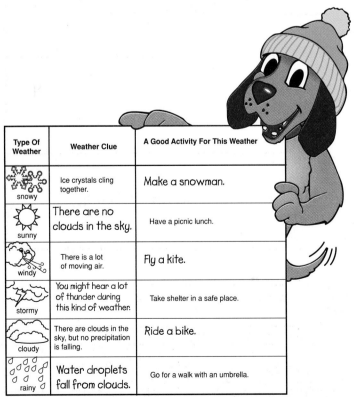

Type Of Weather	Weather Clue	A Good Activity For This Weather
snowy	Ice crystals cling together.	Make a snowman.
sunny	There are no clouds in the sky.	Have a picnic lunch.
windy	There is a lot of moving air.	Fly a kite.
stormy	You might hear a lot of thunder during this kind of weather.	Take shelter in a safe place.
cloudy	There are clouds in the sky, but no precipitation is falling.	Ride a bike.
rainy	Water droplets fall from clouds.	Go for a walk with an umbrella.

NaNName _____

Identifying types of weather

Oh, The Weather Outside...

Cut.
Glue and write to complete the chart.

Type Of Weather	Weather Clue	A Good Activity For This Weather
	Ice crystals cling together.	
		Have a picnic lunch.
	There is a lot of moving air.	
		Take shelter in a safe place.
	There are clouds in the sky, but no precipitation is falling.	
		Go for a walk with an umbrella.

Bonus Box: What is your favorite type of weather? Write about it on the back of this sheet. Add a picture.

©1998 The Education Center, Inc. • *Lifesaver Lessons*™ • Grade 2 • TEC509

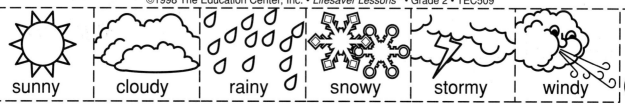

sunny   cloudy   rainy   snowy   stormy   windy   5

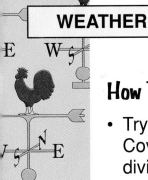

How To Extend The Lesson:

• Try this class bulletin-board activity for a seasonal approach to weather! Cover a bulletin board with brightly colored paper. Use a marker or yarn to divide it into quarters, and label each section with the name of a season. Then have youngsters create seasonal collages by cutting out pictures from discarded magazines and mounting them on the bulletin board in the appropriate sections. After everyone has contributed to the display, invite students to describe the types of weather depicted for each season. Record their responses for each time of year on a small separate sheet of chart paper, and mount the paper beside the corresponding section of the display.

• Long ago, many people used weather legends and sayings to help them remember natural signs of weather changes. Share with youngsters several of these sayings, such as the ones below.

— When dew is on the grass, rain will never come to pass.
— Flies will swarm before a storm.
— Red sky at night, sailors' delight; red sky in the morning, sailors take warning.

Engage students in a discussion about these sayings. Do youngsters believe that they accurately forecast the weather? How could they find out? No doubt your young meteorologists will be eager to put these legends to the test!

• Have each student record her weather observations in a weather log! Instruct her to staple a desired number of sheets of paper between two construction-paper covers and to personalize the cover. Direct her to make daily entries in her log by drawing and writing about the day's weather conditions. Also have her draw in a corner of each page the corresponding international weather symbol (refer to the chart shown). For added learning fun, have each youngster keep a log at several different times during the year and compare the recorded weather conditions.

International Weather Symbols	
❜	light drizzle
⠢	steady, heavy rain
✳	light snow
✳✳	steady, light snow
⬋	lightning
6	hurricane
○	no clouds
◑	half covered with clouds
●	completely overcast

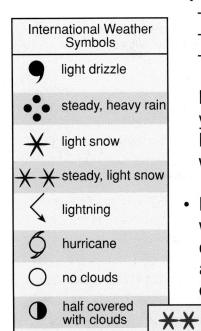

✳✳ December 16

It snowed all day.
I made a snowman!

Seasonal Search

Creativity springs forth as youngsters explore the seasons!

> **Skill:** Identifying seasonal attributes

Estimated Lesson Time: 40 minutes

Teacher Preparation:
1. On the chalkboard, write the four lists shown at the bottom of page 8. Be sure to write the words in the exact order shown.
2. Duplicate page 9 for each student.

Materials:
1 copy of page 9 per student
crayons

Background Information:
An area's typical weather pattern is known as its *climate.* The area near the equator has a tropical climate, and the Arctic and Antarctic have a polar climate. Neither of these climates changes much during the year. In contrast, the areas that have a temperate climate (located between the equator and the poles) experience noticeable weather changes throughout the year. They usually have warm, dry summers and cold, wet winters. These seasonal changes are caused by the Earth's tilting toward or away from the Sun. When it is summer in the Northern Hemisphere, it is winter in the Southern Hemisphere. Some of the characteristics of each season in the Northern Hemisphere are described below.

Spring: This season begins about March 21. Increasing temperatures, new leaves and flowers, and animals coming out of hibernation are evident during spring.
Summer: This is the warmest season, and it begins about June 21. Flowers and plants flourish and fruit ripens during the summer.
Autumn: This season begins about September 21. In autumn the weather cools; deciduous trees change color and lose their leaves.
Winter: This is the coldest season, and it begins about December 21. Most plants rest during the winter months, causing many landscapes to look bare.

Introducing The Lesson:

Read with students the words listed on the chalkboard. Challenge young-sters to determine how the words are grouped in columns. Help students reach the conclusion that the words are grouped by season—autumn, winter, spring, and summer, respectively. Invite students to identify listed words that could belong in more than one seasonal category, and have them explain their reasoning.

Steps:

1. Use the Background Information on page 7 to explain where and why seasonal changes occur.

2. Describe some of the attributes of each season. Invite youngsters to name additional characteristics.

3. Tell students that each of them will use this information to create a seasonal word search for a classmate to solve.

4. Give each student a copy of page 9. Instruct her to use her favorite season for the activity. Each youngster completes the sentences by writing an appropriate answer in each blank on her sheet. Then she writes each of these words either horizontally or vertically in the grid at the bottom. (If a student has a two-word answer, instruct her not to leave a blank between the two words.) She fills in the remaining squares with random letters.

5. Have each youngster trade her completed puzzle with a classmate and ask him to solve it by lightly coloring or circling with crayons the featured words.

6. Ask students to return their papers to the owners and have the creator of each word search verify her classmate's solution.

7. For an added challenge, have students complete the Bonus Box activity.

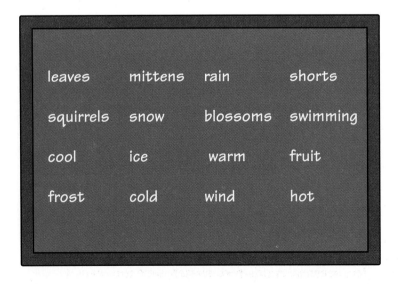

leaves	mittens	rain	shorts
squirrels	snow	blossoms	swimming
cool	ice	warm	fruit
frost	cold	wind	hot

Name _____

Seasonal Search

Choose a season.
Complete each sentence to tell about it.

1. The name of the season is _____.

2. The temperature during this season is usually _____.

3. The weather during this season is usually _____.

4. _____ is a month in this season.

5. During this season you can _____ and _____.

6. Two types of clothing for this season are _____ and _____.

7. In this season you will see _____ and _____.

Write each answer on the grid below.
Fill in the rest of the squares with different letters.
Trade papers with a classmate and have him or her find the words.

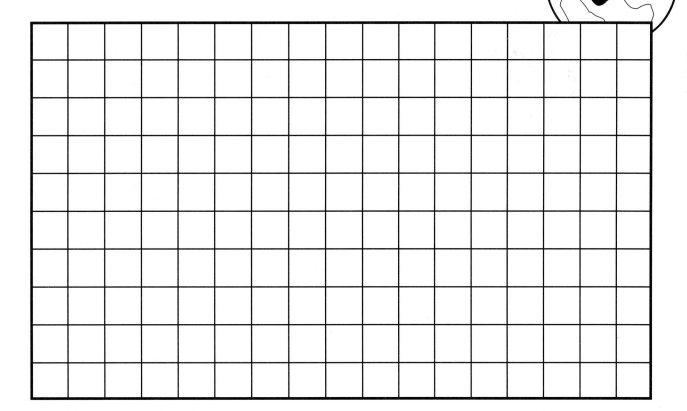

Bonus Box: On the back of this sheet, list the four seasons. Beside each season, write two words that tell about its weather.

How To Extend The Lesson:

- For a fun science-based writing activity, have youngsters create seasonal flip books. To make a booklet cover, a student folds a sheet of 9" x 12" construction paper in half, keeping the fold at the top. Next she folds in half two or three sheets of blank paper. She slides the folded paper inside the booklet cover and staples the resulting 9" x 6" booklet near the fold. On one cover she writes the name of her favorite season. Then she lifts the cover and writes about this season on the front of each booklet page. Encourage her to include information from her word search, such as the typical temperature and weather. Next have each student turn over her booklet and write the name of her least favorite season on the other cover. Instruct her to lift this cover and write about the corresponding time of year. (This story will be written on the back of her first story.) Give students an opportunity to share their completed books before showcasing them in the classroom library. Youngsters will surely flip over these creative-writing projects!

- A love of literature will blossom any time of year with these seasonal selections!
  — *Ox-Cart Man* by Donald Hall (Puffin Books, 1983)
  — *What A Wonderful Day To Be A Cow* by Carolyn Lesser (Alfred A. Knopf Books For Young Readers, 1995)
  — *The Seasons And Someone* by Virginia Kroll (Harcourt Brace & Company, 1994)
  — *The Reasons For Seasons* by Gail Gibbons (Holiday House, Inc.; 1996)

Winter

Weather	Clothing	Animals & Plants	Activities
cold	jackets	bears hibernate	skiing
icy	hats		sledding
snowy	mittens	thicker fur	making snowmen
stormy		bare trees	
frosty			

- Reinforce students' understanding of seasons with this vocabulary-building activity! Write the four seasons on separate sheets of bulletin-board paper. Divide each sheet into four columns and label each column with a different category as shown. Then focusing on one season per day, have youngsters brainstorm words for each category as you record their ideas in the corresponding columns. Display the lists in an accessible area of your classroom. As you continue to explore the topic of weather with students, record additional information. Encourage youngsters to refer to these growing vocabulary lists throughout the year.

Fall For Temperature

*This red-hot lesson teaches students that
reading thermometers is really cool!*

Skill: Reading and interpreting Fahrenheit thermometers

Estimated Lesson Time: 45 minutes

Teacher Preparation:
1. On the chalkboard, draw four simple thermometer shapes without scales. Shade the thermometers to represent the following temperatures: hot, warm, cool, and cold.
2. Cut one 1 1/2" x 12" strip of red paper for each student.
3. Write a different temperature on each of ten or more index cards.
4. Duplicate page 13 for each student.

Materials:
1 copy of page 13 per student
one 1 1/2" x 12" strip of red paper per student
ten or more index cards, each programmed with a different temperature
stapler
scissors

Background Information:
- Thermometers—the most common type of weather instrument—not only help people determine appropriate clothing for each day, but they also provide information about variations in weather patterns. Temperatures are usually lowest just before dawn. They peak in the afternoon, then fall. Any discrepancies in this pattern indicate that the weather is about to change.

- In 1612 Galileo made the first thermometer with colored alcohol and a glass tube. He based this invention on his discovery that liquids expand when warmed. During the next 200 years, scientists experimented with the design of thermometers by using many different liquids, including wine. Mercury is now the most commonly used substance for thermometers because it results in the most accurate readings. Thermometer readings were standardized in 1714, when Gabriel Daniel Fahrenheit created the first widely used thermometer scale. On this scale, the freezing point of water is 32° and its boiling point is 212°.

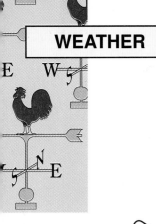

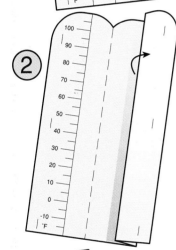

Introducing The Lesson:

Direct students' attention to the thermometers on the chalkboard. Ask them to identify the thermometer that represents a hot temperature; then write the word *hot* below it. Continue in a like manner with *cold,* then *warm* and *cool.* Discuss with youngsters the subjectivity of these terms. Explain that this lesson will teach each of them how to read a thermometer with a standard numerical scale.

Steps:

1. Share the Background Information on page 11 with students.

2. On one of the thermometers on the chalkboard, add a scale with marks at five- and ten-degree intervals and labels at ten-degree intervals. Help students use the scale to determine the temperature shown.

3. Give students additional practice reading a thermometer by increasing or decreasing the shaded area on this thermometer and having them identify the corresponding temperature. With students' help, write the new temperature below the thermometer.

4. Tell youngsters that each of them will make a thermometer. Distribute a copy of page 13, a strip of red paper, and scissors to each student.

5. Each child cuts his pattern on the heavy dark lines. Then, on one of the dotted lines, he folds the paper toward the middle. Next he folds back the resulting flap on the solid line. (See the illustrations.) He repeats these steps with the other dotted and solid lines.

6. Have each youngster staple his folded paper on the staple lines and insert his paper strip between the two folded sections as shown.

7. Announce that students will represent different temperatures with the resulting thermometers. Display a programmed index card; then have a volunteer read it aloud and describe the temperature as hot, warm, cool, or cold. Have each student move his paper strip up or down to correspond with this temperature; then verify youngsters' responses.

8. Repeat this activity in a similar manner with the remaining index cards and different student volunteers.

Pattern
Use with Steps 4, 5, 6, 7, and 8 on page 12.

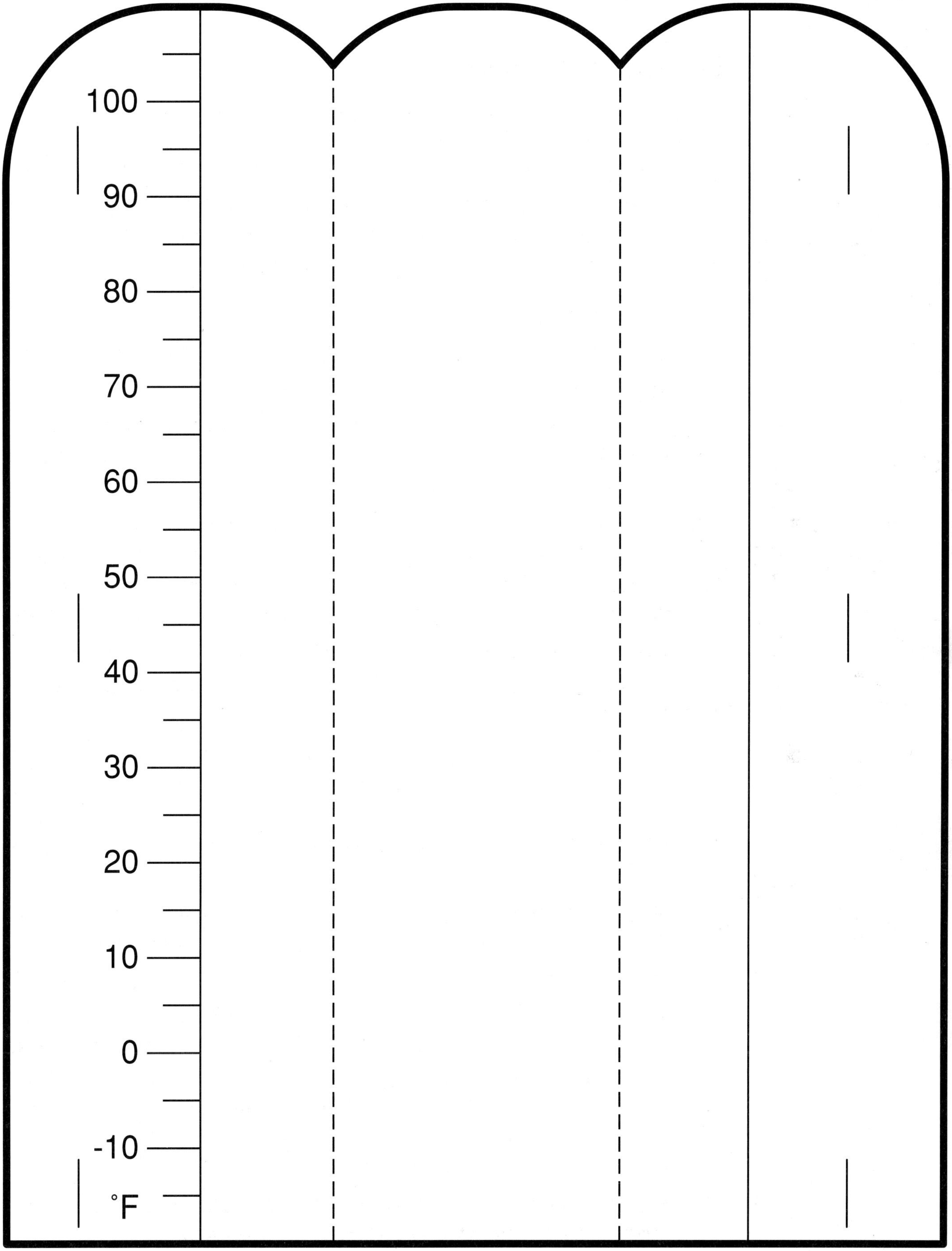

100
90
80
70
60
50
40
30
20
10
0
-10
°F

©1998 The Education Center, Inc. • *Lifesaver Lessons*™ • Grade 2 • TEC509

13

How To Extend The Lesson:

• Have youngsters use their paper thermometers for this weather-wise activity! Give each youngster a paper card that has been programmed with a different temperature. Have him adjust the paper strip of his thermometer to correspond with this temperature. Next direct him to fold a sheet of white paper in half and then unfold it. Have him cut out and shade a copy of the thermometer pattern shown and then glue it onto one side of his paper. On the other side, instruct him to draw an activity or outdoor scene that is appropriate for the temperature shown. Then have students group and sequence their completed drawings by temperature (from coldest to hottest) and mount them on a classroom or hall wall to create an eye-catching display.

• Incorporate addition and subtraction into your study of thermometers. To prepare for this activity, place an outdoor thermometer in an easily accessible location on your school grounds. Each morning select a student at random to read the thermometer and record the temperature on a class chart or bar graph. Ask another youngster to read and record the temperature in the afternoon. Then challenge students to determine the difference. After several days, have youngsters analyze the data that they have collected and invite them to make predictions based on this information. Remind students that any variations in the typical temperature pattern indicate upcoming changes in the weather.

• Students will love this nifty center activity! Program each of several index cards with a different temperature. Color a copy of the thermometer pattern shown to correspond with each temperature; then cut it out and glue it onto a blank index card. Code the back of each temperature and thermometer card for self-checking. Shuffle the prepared cards and place them in a container in a center. A student reads each temperature card and pairs it with the corresponding thermometer card. He then flips the cards to check his work. After completing the center, he prepares it for the next student by shuffling the cards and returning them to the container.

100
90
80
70
60
50
40
30
20
10
0
-10
°F

Everything's Coming Up Pumpkins!

*Plant a seed of knowledge with this life-cycle lesson
and harvest a bumper crop of learning fun!*

Skill: Sequencing the life-cycle stages of a pumpkin

Estimated Lesson Time: 30 minutes

Teacher Preparation:
Duplicate page 17 for each student.

Materials:
1 copy of page 17 per student
one 12" x 18" sheet of construction paper per student
crayons
scissors
glue

Background Information:
Pumpkins begin as small white seeds that are planted approximately one inch deep in soil. After several days, roots begin to grow downward and stems grow upward. After the stems break through the soil, two *seed leaves* appear where each seed was planted. Next, jagged-edged leaves called *pumpkin vine leaves* quickly grow and stems twist along the ground as they become vines. On the vines, curly tendrils appear and yellow flowers bloom. Below some of the flowers, tiny green bulbs grow. They slowly turn from green to orange and become ripened pumpkins. This process from seed to mature pumpkin takes about four months. If the seeds from a mature pumpkin are planted, the cycle will begin again.

Introducing The Lesson:

Write the word *pumpkin* on the right side of the chalkboard and draw a simple picture of a pumpkin beside it. Invite youngsters to describe a fully grown pumpkin while you record their responses below the word *pumpkin*. Next ask youngsters to tell where pumpkins come from. Verify that pumpkins come from seeds; then write and illustrate the word *seed* on the left side of the chalkboard. Have students tell what a pumpkin seed looks like while you write their descriptions below the word *seed*. Invite youngsters to predict some of the changes that occur as a small pumpkin seed develops into a large orange pumpkin. Accept all responses and write them between the words *seed* and *pumpkin*. Tell students that they will learn about a pumpkin's life cycle with this lesson.

Steps:

1. Use the Background Information on page 15 to describe to youngsters the life-cycle stages of a pumpkin. Then have students orally compare and contrast this information with their ideas recorded on the chalkboard. Erase the chalkboard after this discussion.

2. Give each student a copy of page 17, a 12" x 18" sheet of construction paper, crayons, scissors, and glue. Tell youngsters that each of them will use these materials to create a poster of a pumpkin's life cycle.

3. Read with students the sentences on page 17. Then list the following words on the chalkboard: *orange, flower, stem, vine, bulb,* and *root*.

4. Have each student use the listed words to complete the sentences on his sheet. Then direct him to color and cut out each box and to personalize the cover.

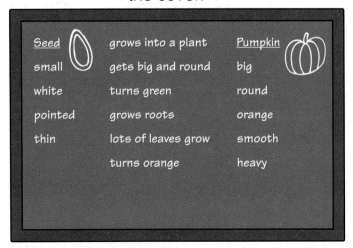

5. Next instruct each youngster to fold and cut his sheet of construction paper in half lengthwise. Have him glue the two resulting pieces together to make one long strip and then sequence and glue the boxes onto the strip.

6. Have youngsters orally summarize a pumpkin's life-cycle stages and then display their completed posters in the classroom or hall.

Everything's Coming Up PUMPKINS!

Name _____

Next the stem grows into a
_____. Leaves grow, too.

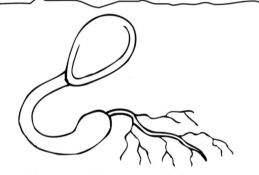

A pumpkin seed is planted. Its
_____ grows downward, and
its _____ grows upward.

The pumpkin slowly turns
_____ and is ready to pick.

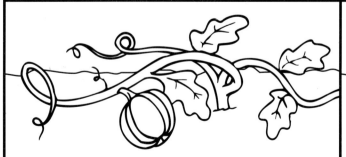

A small green _____ grows
from the flower.

A yellow _____ blooms on
the vine.

How To Extend The Lesson:

• Explain to students that most plants, including pumpkins, need sunlight, water, soil, and air. Then have each youngster conduct an experiment with a partner to determine how the amount of one of these needs—sunlight—affects plants. To do this, each student pair plants fast-germinating seeds, such as radish seeds, in two different containers. (The containers should have the same amount and same kind of soil.) Then each twosome places one container in a sunny location and the other in a dark location, waters them the same way, and predicts what will happen. At the end of a designated period of time, invite youngsters to share their results and compare them with their predictions. If desired, conduct similar experiments varying the amount of water, soil, and air that plants receive.

• Reinforce students' understanding of a pumpkin's life cycle with this creative-writing activity! Begin by reading aloud a book about pumpkins, such as *The Pumpkin Patch* by Elizabeth King (Viking Penguin, 1996) or *Too Many Pumpkins* by Linda White (Holiday House, Inc.; 1996). Then have youngsters write a story with the following story starter: "Peter LaPlante wanted to grow a perfect pumpkin to enter in the state fair. So one day…." Encourage them to use the information they've learned from the lesson on page 17 and from the book just shared in their stories. Direct students to illustrate their completed stories; then display your young authors' work on a bulletin board titled "Presenting The Perfect Pumpkin."

Group Number	Circumference of Pumpkin	Number of Seeds	
		Prediction	Actual
1	20"	100	
2	24"	150	
3	30"	110	
4	18"	60	
5	22"	50	
6	24"	75	
7	17"	40	

• Remind youngsters that a pumpkin's life cycle begins with a seed. Divide youngsters into small groups, assign each group a number, and give it a pumpkin. Then have each group measure the circumference of its pumpkin. Divide a sheet of chart paper into four columns, and record each pumpkin's circumference as shown. Next have each group predict how many seeds its pumpkin has and record its prediction. Cut off the top of each group's pumpkin; then have the group members take turns using a large spoon to scoop out the seeds. Record the actual number of seeds for each pumpkin; then discuss the results. How does the pumpkin's size correspond with the number of seeds? Does the pumpkin with the largest circumference have the most seeds? If desired, use these seeds for additional science explorations. Or clean and bake them for a nutritious snack!

Focus On Flowers!

Student learning will blossom with this "plant-astic" lesson!

Skill: Identifying the parts of a flower

Estimated Lesson Time: 25 minutes

Teacher Preparation:
1. On the chalkboard, draw a simple diagram of a flower. Use the illustration on page 20 as a reference, but do not include the labels.
2. Duplicate page 21 for each student.

Materials:
colored chalk
1 copy of page 21 per student

Background Information:

Many plants have flowers. Flowers are important because they hold seeds—the beginnings of new plants. Several other parts of flowers that are important to the reproductive cycle of plants are described below.

- **Petals:** Petals shelter the reproductive parts of a flower. Some petals are brightly colored or have markings to attract insects for pollination.

- **Pistil:** The pistil is a tube in the middle of the flower.

- **Stigma:** The stigma is the sticky part at the top of a pistil.

- **Stamens:** The stamens are the stalks surrounding the pistil.

- **Anther:** The anther is the tip of a stamen. Anthers produce a yellow powder called *pollen*.

In order for a flower to reproduce, pollen from its stamen needs to be transferred to the stigma of a flower of the same type. This process—*pollination*—occurs in different ways. For example, wind may blow pollen from flower to flower, or insects may carry pollen on their bodies from one flower to another. After pollination, a long tube grows through the pistil into an *ovule*. This is the beginning of a seed. Fruit grows around the seed. When the fruit ripens, the seeds are ready to develop into new plants, and the reproductive cycle continues.

Introducing The Lesson:

Ask students to think about why many flower petals are brightly colored or have markings. Give youngsters an opportunity to share their ideas; then explain that the appearance of petals attracts certain insects that are important to the process of pollination. Explain to students that pollination is necessary for new plants to be created. Then tell students that this lesson will teach them about some of the flower parts that play a role in this process.

Steps:

1. Direct students' attention to the diagram on the chalkboard. Use the relevant part of the Background Information on page 19 to explain each of the following flower parts: petals, pistil, stamens, anthers, and stigma. As you introduce each part, outline it on the diagram with colored chalk and label it (refer to the illustration below).

2. Describe pollen and indicate on the diagram where it is located on a flower. Then use the last paragraph of the Background Information to review the process of pollination.

3. Give each student a copy of page 21. Have her refer to the chalkboard diagram and use the information you have presented to mark the illustration as indicated and complete the sentences on her sheet.

4. Challenge students to complete the Bonus Box activity.

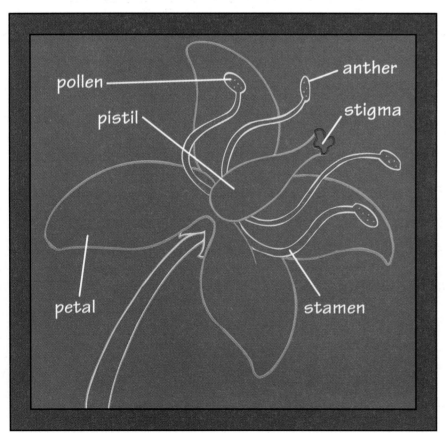

Focus On Flowers!

Read each sentence.
Follow the directions.

Trace the **petals** with a red crayon.

Make a check mark on each **stamen**.

Trace the **pistil** with a black crayon.

Circle the **stigma**.

Mark one **anther** with an X.

Color yellow **pollen** on one anther.

Complete each sentence.
Use the Word Bank.

1. The _____ is a tube in the middle of a flower.

2. Some _____ attract insects with bright colors.

3. The stalks around a pistil are called _____.

4. The sticky part at the top of a pistil is a _____.

5. The _____ is the tip of a stamen.

6. Anthers make a yellow powder called _____.

Word Bank					
pistil	stamens	pollen	stigma	petals	anther

Bonus Box: On the back of this sheet, write two ways that pollen can be transferred from one flower to another.

How To Extend The Lesson:

• Obtain one flower for every two or three students in your class. For best results, acquire a few different types. Give each student group an opportunity to examine its flower and share observations. Then review each of the basic flower parts with youngsters while they find them on their flowers. Tell students that during this lesson they will examine petals more closely. Assign each group a number. Then on a large sheet of paper, make a chart with the following column headings: Group, Color, Markings, Shape, and Number (the last four columns refer to petal characteristics). Add other columns and headings as desired. Have each group examine its flower for the listed characteristics and share them with the class. Then record each group's information on the chart. Lead youngsters in a discussion about the completed chart. What do they notice? How does the number of petals compare for flowers that are the same type? Different types? How about the shape of each petal? No doubt youngsters' observation skills will bloom with this hands-on activity!

• Your young botanists' love of literature will grow with these terrific titles!
 —*The Tiny Seed* by Eric Carle (Simon & Schuster Children's Division, 1991)
 —*Miss Rumphius* by Barbara Cooney (Puffin Books, 1985)
 —*The Rose In My Garden* by Arnold Lobel (William Morrow & Co., Inc.; 1993)

stigma

the sticky part at the top of a pistil

• Reinforce flower-part identification skills with this center game for partners! Write the basic flower parts on separate paper cards. Then write a corresponding clue or definition for each of these words on another card. Shuffle the cards and place them in a container at a center. Each student pair places the cards facedown on a playing surface. In turn each player turns over two cards. If a word and a matching definition (or clue) are shown, he keeps the cards. If the cards do not match, he returns them to their original positions. Play continues until all of the cards have been correctly paired. The player who has the most cards at the end of the game is the winner. The players then shuffle the cards and return them to the container to prepare the center for other students.

Absolutely "Tree-rific!"

Students' appreciation of trees will take root with this valuable learning activity!

Skill: Recognizing the value of trees

Estimated Lesson Time: 25 minutes

Teacher Preparation:

1. Write the following words on the chalkboard: "furniture," "chocolate," "soap," and "bulletin boards."
2. Divide a sheet of bulletin-board paper into two columns. Label one column "Products" and the other column "Benefits."
3. Duplicate page 25 for each student.

Materials:

1 labeled sheet of bulletin-board paper
1 copy of page 25 per student
crayons

Background Information:

Trees are among the most useful plants. Some of the many products and benefits of trees are listed below.

- **Products**
  - **Food:** Trees are a source of food for people as well as animals. They provide many different types of food, such as fruits, chocolate, and nuts.
  - **Wood:** Wood products made from trees include furniture, houses, paper, and cardboard.
  - **Sap:** Sap from some trees is used to make maple syrup, chewing gum, and soap.
  - **Bark:** Some tree bark is used to make bottle stoppers or bulletin boards.
- **Benefits**
  - **Soil And Water Conservation:** Trees act as windbreaks in some areas, and their roots hold soil in place, keeping it from washing away in heavy rains or floods. Tree roots also store water in the ground.
  - **Air:** Trees help keep the balance of gases in the air by absorbing carbon dioxide and producing oxygen.
  - **Shelter/Recreation:** Forests provide shelter for many animals and recreational areas for people. They also offer shade and beautify our landscapes.

Introducing The Lesson:

Direct students' attention to the words on the chalkboard. Challenge youngsters to determine what the listed items have in common. Lead them to the conclusion that furniture, chocolate, soap, and bulletin boards are products from wood, seeds, sap, and bark, respectively. Tell students that trees are very useful to people and animals, and that this lesson will explore additional products and benefits of these plants.

Products	Benefits
fruit	produce oxygen
maple syrup	give shade
bottle stoppers	homes for animals
furniture	hold soil in place
cardboard	make yards pretty
paper	fun to climb
chewing gum	windbreaks

Steps:

1. Share the Background Information on page 23.

2. Show students the prepared chart. Ask students to brainstorm products and benefits of trees and identify the listed category in which each of these belong. Record youngsters' ideas in the appropriate columns on the chart.

3. Give each student a copy of page 25. Have her use the Word Bank to complete the sentences and label the pictures on her sheet.

4. Challenge youngsters to complete the Bonus Box activity. If desired provide an opportunity for students to share this work with classmates.

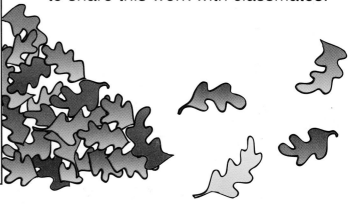

Name _____

Absolutely "Tree-rific!"

Use the Word Bank to complete each sentence.
Label each picture on the tree with the matching word.
Color the pictures.

Word Bank

soap   fruits   yards   roots
shade   homes

1. Trees give us _____ on a hot day.

2. Some trees grow _____ for us to eat.

3. Tree _____ hold soil in place.

4. Some animals make their _____ in trees.

5. Sap from some trees is used to make _____.

6. Trees make our _____ look pretty.

Bonus Box: On the back of this sheet, list ten products that come from trees.

©1998 The Education Center, Inc. • *Lifesaver Lessons*™ • Grade 2 • TEC509 • Key p. 95

25

PLANTS

How To Extend The Lesson:

• Trees and other types of plants provide many valuable products. For example, trees provide lumber for building homes, and the bark from some trees is used for medicinal purposes. Food is obtained from several different parts of plants, such as seeds, roots, leaves, flower buds, and fruits. And cotton is one plant product that is used to make clothing. Discuss these and other plant products with youngsters; then divide students into small groups. Have each group compile a list titled "We thank plants for…." If desired challenge youngsters to categorize the items on their lists. Give each group an opportunity to share its work; then mount students' completed lists on a classroom wall.

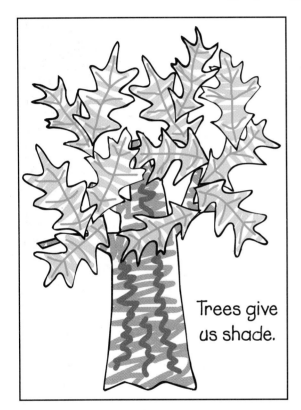

Trees give us shade.

• What better way to teach youngsters about caring for our natural resources than with engaging literature? Read aloud *The Lorax* by Dr. Seuss (Random House Books For Young Readers, 1971). Then discuss how the Once-ler's factory affected plant life and other aspects of the environment. Ask each child to write a letter to the Once-ler expressing how he feels about the impact of the Thneed factory. Encourage students to give the Once-ler suggestions for taking better care of natural resources. To conclude this activity, have each student imagine that he is in charge of the last Truffula seed and discuss what he would do with it.

• Highlight the importance of trees with this "tree-mendous" bulletin-board activity! Take students outside to a wooded area. Direct each youngster to use a brown crayon and a sheet of drawing paper to make a rubbing of tree bark. Then have each student find one or two leaves that have fallen to the ground and take them back to the classroom with his crayon rubbing. Next each student makes several leaf rubbings with a green crayon and drawing paper. Direct each student to create a likeness of a tree by cutting out his rubbings and gluing them onto a sheet of paper. Have each youngster write on his paper one reason that trees are important. Mount students' completed work on a brightly colored bulletin board titled "Trees Are Tops!" With this creative display, it's easy to see that trees are tops!

Home, Sweet, Home

Whether it's a nest, log, or cave, there's no place like home!

Skill: Identifying animal habitats

Estimated Lesson Time: 25 minutes

Teacher Preparation:
Duplicate page 29 for each student.

Materials:
1 copy of page 29 per student
1 sheet of chart paper per student group
several real estate ads (optional)
scissors
glue
crayons

Background Information:

Every animal is suited to live in a particular environment or habitat. Information about the seven major types of habitats is provided below.

- **Mountains:** Mountain habitats range from dense forests to bare, rocky ground. Bears and tigers are among the animals that live at the forested bases of some mountains. Birds of prey and mountain goats are found on mountains at higher altitudes.
- **Grasslands:** Few trees grow in the grasslands because of insufficient rainfall or ground that is too sandy. Giraffes, elephants, and lions live in the grasslands of Africa, also known as the African savannah.
- **Temperate Forests:** Temperate forests have many deciduous and evergreen trees. Animals that live in this habitat include chipmunks, owls, and salamanders.
- **Tropical Forests:** In these forests near the equator, it is very hot and it rains frequently. Anteaters, chimpanzees, and a large number of insects make their homes in this habitat.
- **Deserts:** Deserts are extremely dry. Some deserts are vast areas of sand, but others are rocky regions. Camels, geckos, and scorpions live in deserts.
- **Polar Regions:** These areas in the Arctic and Antarctica are bitterly cold. Winters in the polar regions are stormy and dark. The summers are short and there is daylight nearly 24 hours a day. Polar bears, walruses, and puffins make their homes in the polar regions.
- **Oceans:** The oceans and seas are the largest natural habitat and are heavily populated by creatures such as blue whales, dolphins, and starfish.

Introducing The Lesson:

Ask youngsters to brainstorm words, such as *hilly* or *flat,* that describe the areas in which they live; record them on the chalkboard. Explain that animals are similar to people in that each of them lives in a particular type of environment. Unlike people, though, some animals can live only in one type of environment because they are uniquely suited to its special features and cannot survive in a different location. Tell students that they will learn about several different animal habitats, or environments, in this lesson.

Steps:

1. Use the Background Information on page 27 to describe to students the seven major habitats and some of the animals that live in them.

2. Divide students into seven groups and assign each group a different habitat. On a large sheet of chart paper, have each group write the name of its assigned habitat and a list of animals that live in it.

3. Have each group share its completed list; then display the lists in the classroom for reference.

4. Read aloud some real estate ads or the ads shown on this page. Discuss with students how special features of homes are highlighted in this type of ad.

5. Give each student a copy of page 29. Explain that on this sheet each habitat is described in a brief real estate ad. Have each student color and cut out his animal pictures. Next read each ad with students as they glue the pictures beside the appropriate ads. Remind students to use the Background Information and the group lists as references.

6. For added learning fun, challenge students to complete the Bonus Box activity.

Excellent Location
Furnished two-bedroom house with a screened-in porch. Air conditioning and new appliances. Close to shopping center.

Lake Area
Three bedrooms, two baths. Brick home in rural area. Seven rooms, new carpet, fenced yard, and patio. Walking distance to lake.

Home, Sweet Home

Color and cut out each animal card.
Read each habitat ad.
Glue each animal card beside the matching ad.

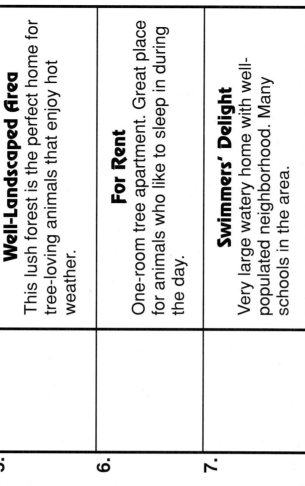

1.

For Sale

A high-rise home atop a rocky mountain. Perfect for surefooted animals that love to graze.

2.

Available For Immediate Occupancy!

Large home in dry, sandy location. If you like hot weather and you store your own water, this is the place for you!

3.

Cool Home!

Icy waterfront home for sale. Great for strong swimmers that love to eat fish.

4.

Spacious Home

Looking for a home in a wide-open area? If so, this grassy home is for you!

5.

Well-Landscaped Area

This lush forest is the perfect home for tree-loving animals that enjoy hot weather.

6.

For Rent

One-room tree apartment. Great place for animals who like to sleep in during the day.

7.

Swimmers' Delight

Very large watery home with well-populated neighborhood. Many schools in the area.

Bonus Box: Choose one of the seven habitats. On the back of this sheet, draw and label a picture of it with at least three animals that live there.

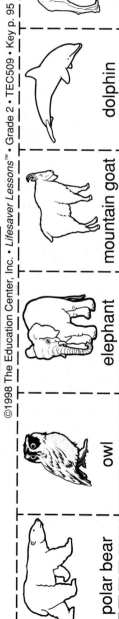

| polar bear | owl | elephant | mountain goat | dolphin | camel | chimpanzee |

How To Extend The Lesson:

• Any youngster who has ever asked his parent for a pet will readily identify with Brian—the main character of *The Salamander Room* by Anne Mazer (Alfred A. Knopf Books For Young Readers, 1994). Brian wants to keep a salamander for a pet, but his mother doesn't seem to like this idea. In response to her questions about how he will care for it, Brian envisions transforming his bedroom into the perfect salamander habitat—complete with trees, frogs, and birds. Share this imaginative story with youngsters; then ask each student to name the animal she would most like to have. Next direct each youngster to write and illustrate a story about how she would provide an appropriate environment and good care for her pet. Bind students' completed work with a cover, and title the resulting book *Our Perfect Pet-Care Guide.*

• Youngsters will love being habitat detectives with this clue-filled activity! Cut a class supply of paper strips and program each strip with the name of a different animal. Then place the programmed strips in a large container. To play, each student in turn takes a strip from the container and silently reads the corresponding animal name. He orally gives clues about this animal's home and habitat, and challenges his classmates to identify the described animal. After they name the correct animal, the activity continues in a similar manner until every youngster has taken a turn.

• Students will be right at home with this creative class-book project! Read aloud *A House Is A House For Me* by Mary Ann Hoberman (Puffin Books, 1993), an inviting book that presents a variety of houses from a unique perspective. After sharing this delightful story, have students brainstorm animals and their homes as you record their responses on a chart (similar to the one shown). Next instruct students to use the list to create a class book. To do this, each student selects one animal and, on a sheet of paper, writes and illustrates a sentence about its home, using Hoberman's book as a model. Then, on another sheet of paper, a student volunteer draws a picture of the class and writes "And a school is a house for us." Using this sheet as the last page, bind all of the completed pages with a cover. No doubt your classroom library will be the perfect house for this student-made book!

Animals	Homes
beaver	lodge
grizzly bear	cave
chicken	coop
sheep	fold
cow and horse	barn
rabbit	hutch
centipede and beetle	rotting log
chipmunk and mole	underground tunnels
ant	hill
bee	hive
mountain lion	den
badger	burrow
raccoon	hollow tree
spider	web
bird	nest
sow	sty

Critter Cover-Ups

*Uncover the facts about fur, feathers, and scales
with this animal classification activity!*

Skill: Classifying animals

Estimated Lesson Time: 25 minutes

Teacher Preparation:
1. Divide a sheet of chart paper into three columns and label each column with one of the following headings: "fur," "feathers," and "scales."
2. Duplicate page 33 for each student.

Materials:
1 sheet of prepared chart paper
1 copy of page 33 per student
crayons

Background Information:
Animals are often classified by common characteristics. For example, animals can be classified by the number of legs they have, their habitats, or how they move. This activity focuses on classifying animals by three types of skin coverings—fur, feathers, and scales.
- **Fur:** Mammals are the only animals that have fur. The fur of mammals, such as cats, dogs, mice, and giraffes, helps retain body heat. Mammal fur varies from the curly wool of sheep, to the stiff short-haired covering of horses.
- **Feathers:** This skin covering is unique to birds. This group of animals includes chickens, parrots, and ducks. Feathers are birds' primary protective coverings. Some male birds have brightly colored or decorative feathers to attract mates. Other birds have feathers that camouflage them in their surroundings.
- **Scales:** The skin of reptiles is covered with scales. Some reptiles, such as lizards and snakes, have one sheet of overlapping scales. Other reptiles, including turtles and crocodiles, have scales that grow in individual areas called *plates*.

Introducing The Lesson:

Write the words "turtle," "owl," and "chicken" on the chalkboard. Challenge students to determine which animal does not belong in this group and to explain their reasoning. Be sure to encourage a variety of responses. For example, youngsters might state that the turtle doesn't belong because it doesn't have feathers, or students might explain that the turtle is different because it has four feet and the other animals do not. Continue in a similar manner with several other groups of three animals—two that have the same type of skin covering and one that does not. (See the list below for examples of animal groups.) Then tell youngsters that with this lesson, they will learn more about one of the ways to group or classify animals—by skin coverings.

Steps:

1. Have youngsters name the skin coverings of the animals discussed in the previous activity—fur, feathers, and scales. Then share with students the Background Information on page 31.

2. Ask students to brainstorm animals that have fur, feathers, or scales. Write each of their responses below the appropriate heading on the prepared chart.

3. Give each student a copy of page 33. With students, review each of the pictured animals and read the directions and questions.

4. Have each youngster color the animals and color the squares to graph her results according to the directions. Then instruct her to answer the questions.

5. Challenge students to complete the Bonus Box activity.

turtle	owl	chicken
fox	mouse	snake
duck	dog	bear
crocodile	snake	cat
giraffe	parrot	fox
snake	bear	turtle

Name _____

Critter Cover-Ups

Look at each animal.
Color it brown if it has **fur**.
Color it blue if it has **feathers**.
Color it green if it has **scales**.
Graph your results below.

Fur	Feathers	Scales

Look at your graph.

1. What type of skin covering do most of the animals have? _____

2. How many of the animals have fur or scales? _____

3. How many of the animals have scales or feathers? _____

4. What group of animals has fur? _____

5. What group of animals has feathers? _____

6. What group of animals has scales? _____

Bonus Box: Choose three animals. On the back of this sheet, write a riddle about each of them. Ask a friend or family member to guess the answers.

33

How To Extend The Lesson:

• Boost students' creativity with this one-of-a-kind animal project! Have each student fold a sheet of drawing paper in half and then unfold it. On one side of the paper, have him create and draw an animal that has fur, feathers, *and* scales. On the other side, instruct each youngster to write the name of his animal and a description of it. Encourage each student to include information about how each of the different types of skin coverings protects his animal. Give each youngster an opportunity to share his completed work, then display these unique projects on a bulletin board titled "Critter Creations."

• Reinforce critical-thinking skills with this open-ended classification activity. Give each student a copy of the pictures below and have her cut them apart. Next ask each youngster to sort her animal pictures by a rule of her choice, such as the number of legs or the type of skin covering. Instruct each student to write her rule and the corresponding animal names on a sheet of paper. Then, in a like manner, ask her to sort her cards by two other rules and record her work. For added learning fun, have each student show a classmate her favorite set of animals and challenge him to determine her sorting rule.

owl	fox	snake	giraffe	duck	bear
turtle	parrot	mouse	crocodile	dinosaur	turkey
flamingo	cat	lion	chicken	lizard	dog

Creepy, Crawly Lotto

Youngsters will go buggy over this insect-identification game!

Skill: Identifying insects

Estimated Lesson Time: 30 minutes

Teacher Preparation:
1. Enlarge the Background Information below. Cut the information about each insect into a strip. Fold each strip in half and place all of the strips in a container.
2. Duplicate page 37 for each student.

Materials:
1 copy of page 37 per student
12 game markers, such as kidney
   beans or buttons, per student
1 enlarged copy of the Background
   Information for the teacher

1 container to hold paper strips
scissors
glue

Background Information:
All insects have six legs and three main body parts. Each insect has a *head*, where eyes, antennae, and jaws are found; a *thorax*, where legs and wings are attached; and an *abdomen*, where food is digested and eggs are produced. Scientists have discovered and named about 1 million insects. Here is information about 12 of them:

- A **dragonfly** can fly backward or hover in one place. As it flies, it holds its legs together, forming a basket for capturing mosquitoes—its prey.
- A **honeybee** is important for pollination. People have collected honey from bees' nests for hundreds of years.
- An **ant** lives in a colony. Most ants make underground nests with many tunnels and rooms.
- A **praying mantis** has a long narrow body and thin legs. Its grasping front legs give it the appearance of praying.
- A **grasshopper** has strong hind legs that are used for jumping and singing.
- A **fly** has only one pair of wings, unlike other insects. Some flies have sticky, hairy pads on their feet to help them walk on smooth, slippery surfaces.
- A **stag beetle** has hardened front wings that cover its hind wings. Its powerful jaws are probably used for fighting.
- A **butterfly** is usually brightly colored and flies during the day. When it rests, it folds its wings upright over its back.
- A **moth** is dull in color and flies at night. When a moth is at rest, it holds its wings flat and rooflike over its body.
- A **walkingstick** is the longest insect. It resembles a twig and blends in with its background.
- A **ladybug** is helpful to gardeners because it eats insects that attack plants.
- A **firefly** makes a bright greenish light that can be seen at night.

Introducing The Lesson:

Ask students to imagine that they are outside and they see an ant, a honeybee, and a butterfly. Ask them to brainstorm the common characteristics of these creatures. Record their responses on the chalkboard. Lead youngsters to the conclusion that these creatures are insects. Use the Background Information on page 35 to explain that all insects have six legs and three main body parts. Tell students that they will learn about 12 different types of insects with this activity.

Steps:

1. Give each student a copy of page 37. Have him cut apart the insect pictures at the bottom of the page and then set aside the lotto board (at the top of the page) for later use.

2. Use the Background Information on page 35 to share with students some of the distinguishing characteristics of one of the pictured insects. Have each student hold up his corresponding picture card. Verify students' responses; then continue in a like manner with the remaining insects.

3. Tell youngsters that they will play a game with their picture cards. Instruct each student to randomly glue his insect pictures onto his lotto board. Then give each youngster game markers.

4. To play the game, take a paper strip from the container and read aloud the information on it without revealing the insect's name. Have each student place a game marker on the corresponding picture on his lotto board.

5. Continue the game in a similar fashion until one student has placed a game marker on each picture in one row. After verifying his marked pictures, declare him the winner of this round.

6. Prepare to play additional rounds in a similar manner by returning all of the strips to the container and having students clear their boards. Each winner becomes the caller for the following round.

Name _____

Creepy, Crawly Lotto

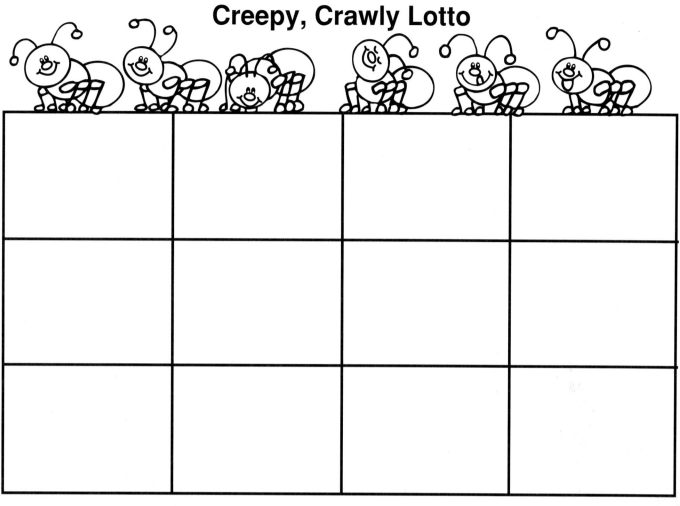

©1998 The Education Center, Inc. • *Lifesaver Lessons*™ • Grade 2 • TEC509

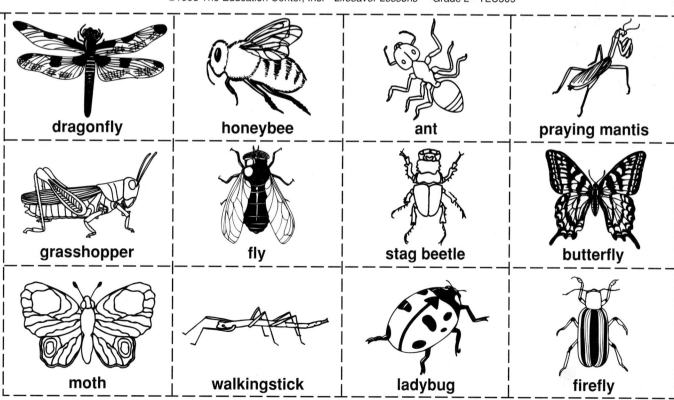

dragonfly	honeybee	ant	praying mantis
grasshopper	fly	stag beetle	butterfly
moth	walkingstick	ladybug	firefly

How To Extend The Lesson:

• Your young entomologists will be all abuzz over this fabulous selection of literature!
— *Bugs!* by David T. Greenberg (Little, Brown And Company; 1997)
— *Night Letters* by Palmyra LoMonaco (Dutton Children's Books, 1996)
— *Insects Are My Life* by Megan McDonald (Orchard Books, 1997)
— *Two Bad Ants* by Chris Van Allsburg (Houghton Mifflin Company, 1988)

• Give students an opportunity to be insect inventors! First remind students that every insect has six legs and three body parts: a head, an abdomen, and a thorax. Also discuss with youngsters the wide variety of insects. For example, a fairy fly is about one-hundredth inch long and can crawl through the eye of a needle. In contrast, the Goliath beetle grows to more than four inches. Not only do insects vary in size, but they also differ in color, markings, and shape. After this discussion, provide students with a selection of colored paper and craft materials, such as glitter, sequins, and buttons. Have each youngster use these supplies to create a poster of a new insect. Instruct her to include her insect's name and a summary of its distinguishing features on her poster. After your inventive students share their completed work, display the posters in the hall for everyone to enjoy. No doubt youngsters will buzz with enthusiasm over this project!

• Integrate math and science with this problem-solving activity. On an index card, write an insect word problem, such as "Jenny sees 18 insect legs. How many insects are there?" Write the answer on the back of the card. Program several other cards in a similar manner. Place them in a large decorated envelope titled "Going Buggy Over Math!" and place the envelope in a center with a supply of blank paper. To use the center, a student takes a card from the envelope, writes and illustrates his solution on a sheet of paper, and checks his work.

Going Buggy Over Math!

Jenny sees 18 insect legs. How many insects are there?

6 6 6

There are 3 insects.

Prehistoric Puzzlers

Your young paleontologists will travel back in time as they solve these remarkable reptile puzzles!

Skill: Identifying different kinds of dinosaurs

Estimated Lesson Time: 30 minutes

Teacher Preparation:
1. Duplicate page 41 for each student.
2. Enlarge and duplicate page 42. Cut apart the dinosaur pictures.

Materials:
1 enlarged copy of page 42 for the teacher
1 copy of page 41 per student
tape

Background Information:
Dinosaurs were reptiles that lived long ago. Most were four-footed plant eaters, but some were meat eaters that walked on their hind legs. There were many types of dinosaurs, and their sizes, shapes, and other distinguishing features varied greatly. Several different kinds of dinosaurs are described below.

- **Herbivores (plant eaters):** Most plant eaters had long necks that helped them reach treetops. Some herbivores had as many as 960 teeth!
  — A **Brachiosaurus** was so tall that it could have looked over a four-story building.
  — A **Stegosaurus** had bony plates on its back. It was as long as two cars, but its brain was only the size of a walnut!
  — An **Ankylosaurus** used its tail as a club to fight enemies. Bony plates covered its back, and sharp spines grew on its sides.
  — A **Triceratops** had a bony frill around the back of its head. It used its three horns to protect itself.
  — An **Apatosaurus** often stood in water to keep safe from its enemies. It used to be known as *Brontosaurus*.
  — An **Ammosaurus** was eight feet long. Its front legs were shorter than its hind legs.
- **Carnivores (meat eaters):** The majority of carnivores walked on their hind legs. Their front limbs were free for catching and holding prey. They had short necks.
  — An **Allosaurus** was twice as tall as a man. It had a ridge along the front of its skull, unlike other meat-eating dinosaurs.
  — A **Tyrannosaurus** had six-inch-long teeth and was a great hunter. It was the largest meat-eating dinosaur.

Introducing The Lesson:

Tell youngsters that they will learn about several types of dinosaurs. Explain that each of these dinosaurs was either a *herbivore* (plant eater) or a *carnivore* (meat eater). Invite youngsters to guess some of the physical characteristics that would have helped each of these types of dinosaurs survive. Then discuss the features of herbivores and carnivores summarized in the Background Information on page 39. For example, herbivorous dinosaurs often had long necks that helped them reach leafy treetops. Most carnivorous dinosaurs walked on their back legs, leaving their front limbs free for catching and holding prey.

Steps:

1. Write the word "herbivores" at the top of one side of the chalkboard and "carnivores" at the top of the other side.

2. Show youngsters a dinosaur picture card from page 42. Have them use what they learned about herbivores and carnivores to guess if the pictured dinosaur ate plants or meat. Then tape the picture card onto the chalkboard under the correct heading.

3. Using the Background Information on page 39, name and describe this dinosaur.

4. Continue classifying and discussing the remaining dinosaurs with youngsters in a like manner.

5. Give each student a copy of page 41. Read the directions, sentences, and each of the dinosaur names with students. Then instruct youngsters to fill in the blanks at the end of each sentence.

6. Challenge students to complete the Bonus Box activity.

Name _____

Prehistoric Puzzlers

Dinosaur Word Bank

brachiosaurus
stegosaurus
ankylosaurus
triceratops
apatosaurus
allosaurus
tyrannosaurus
ammosaurus

Write the name of each dinosaur in the boxes beside the matching clue.
Use the Dinosaur Word Bank.
Cross out each word as you use it.

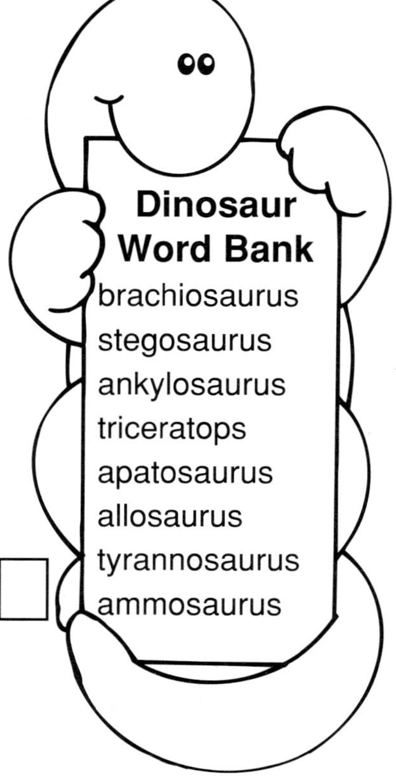

1. This dinosaur often stood in water to keep safe.

2. This plant-eating dinosaur was eight feet long.

3. This meat eater was twice as tall as a man.

4. With six-inch-long teeth, this dinosaur was a great hunter.

5. Bony plates covered the back of this plant-eating dinosaur.

6. This dinosaur used its tail to fight enemies.

7. This plant eater used its three horns to protect itself.

8. This dinosaur could have looked over a four-story building.

Bonus Box: On the back of this sheet, write about your favorite type of dinosaur. Illustrate your work.

How To Extend The Lesson:

• Students will discover what's in a name with this word-building activity! Explain that many dinosaurs are often given names made of root words that describe their shapes, sizes, or other characteristics. For example, stegosaurus means roofed *(stego)* reptile *(saurus)*. On chart paper, display the root words shown below and ask each youngster to use them to invent a new dinosaur name. Then, on a sheet of paper, have him draw and label a dinosaur to correspond with this name. Invite each student to share his completed work. Challenge his classmates to use the root-word list to determine the meaning of this unique reptile's name. No doubt your young "name-asaurs" will have a colossal good time!

alti: tall, high   **mega:** huge   **saurus:** reptile, lizard
bi: two   **mono:** single   **stego:** roofed
bronto: thunder   **ptero:** winged   **stereo:** twin
don, den: tooth   **rex:** king   **top:** head, face
luro: tail   **rhino:** nose   **tri:** three

• A love of literature will never be extinct with "dino-mite" titles like these!
— *An Alphabet Of Dinosaurs* by Peter Dodson (Scholastic Inc., 1995)
— *Can I Have A Stegosaurus, Mom? Can I? Please!?* by Lois Grambling (BridgeWater Books, 1997)
— *How Big Were The Dinosaurs?* by Bernard Most (Harcourt Brace & Company, 1995)

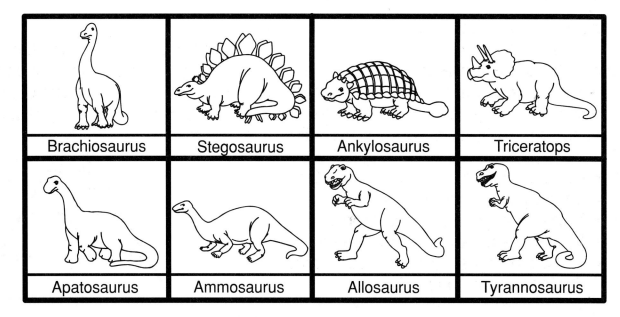

| Brachiosaurus | Stegosaurus | Ankylosaurus | Triceratops |
| Apatosaurus | Ammosaurus | Allosaurus | Tyrannosaurus |

Nutrition News

*Extra! Extra! Read all about it! Second graders make headlines
with nutrition know-how!*

Skill: Interpreting and using the Food Guide Pyramid

Estimated Lesson Time: 45 minutes

Teacher Preparation:
1. Draw the Food Guide Pyramid shown below on a sheet of chart paper.
2. Duplicate page 45 for each student.

Materials:
1 copy of the day's school-lunch menu
1 prepared sheet of chart paper
1 copy of page 45 per student

Background Information:
The U.S. Department of Agriculture used its research about good nutrition to develop the Food Guide Pyramid. This dietary guide outlines a range of daily recommended servings for each major food group. The actual number of servings that a person needs varies depending on how many calories his body requires. Here are examples of foods in each Pyramid category:

- **Fats:** butter, chocolate, mayonnaise
- **Dairy:** yogurt, cheese, milk
- **Protein:** eggs, turkey, chicken
- **Vegetables:** carrots, celery, lettuce
- **Fruits:** oranges, strawberries, apples
- **Grains:** cereal, pasta, bread

Introducing The Lesson:

Tell youngsters that during this lesson, each of them will be an investigative reporter and write about the nutritional value of a school lunch. To begin, have students recall and name the items on the previous day's school menu as you write them on the chalkboard. Explain to students that they will prepare for their investigations by learning about the food groups in which these foods belong.

Steps:

1. Direct students' attention to the Food Guide Pyramid on the prepared chart. Use the Background Information on page 43 to tell students about the different food groups and serving suggestions shown.

2. Have students use the Pyramid to identify the group(s) in which each menu item belongs. Then ask youngsters to determine if the menu includes something from each of the food groups. If it does not, have students suggest additions to the menu. Also ask students how the menu could be changed in order to be more healthful. For example, a baked potato or mashed potatoes could be substituted for potato chips.

3. Erase the chalkboard. Have a student volunteer read today's lunch menu; write it on the chalkboard.

4. Give each student a copy of page 45. On his sheet, have him list each menu item and the food group(s) to which it belongs.

5. Explain to students that newspaper writers share their opinions about the news in editorials. Instruct each youngster to complete the editorial section on his sheet by listing the healthful menu items, then suggesting menu changes to make the lunch even more nutritious. Encourage students to be creative. For instance, a slice of tomato or cheese could be added to a hamburger, or a fresh apple could be substituted for cake.

6. Ask each youngster to draw an illustration of the school lunch in the box provided. Then have him write a short comment or description below it.

7. Challenge students to complete the Bonus Box activity.

8. On a bulletin board titled "Nutrition News," display students' completed work "hot off the press"!

Name _____ *Using the Food Guide Pyramid*

NUTRITION NEWS

Vol. 1   School: _____   Date: _____

▓▓▓▓▓ Graders Investigate School Lunch

Today's Menu   Food Groups

_____   _____

_____   _____

_____   _____

_____   _____

_____   _____

_____   _____

_____   _____

Editorials: How Nutritious Is Our Lunch?

Reporter Lists Healthful Menu Items   **Reporter Suggests Menu Changes**

Bonus Box: On the back of this sheet, write a menu for a nutritious breakfast.

45

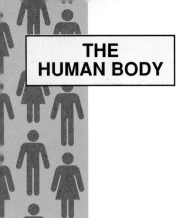

How To Extend The Lesson:

• Make a yummy display of healthful food choices! First, from discarded magazines, have each youngster cut out pictures of healthful foods that together would make a well-balanced, nutritious meal. Then have her glue them onto a paper plate. Cover a bulletin board with a red and white checkered vinyl tablecloth. Mount the completed projects on the bulletin board and add the title "Sink Your Teeth Into Good Nutrition." Now that's a surefire recipe for learning fun!

• Satisfy youngsters' appetites for food-related literature with these tasty titles!
    —*Milo's Great Invention* by Andrew Clements (Steck-Vaughn Company, 1998)
    —*The Seven Silly Eaters* by Mary Ann Hoberman (Harcourt Brace & Company, 1997)
    —*Chocolatina* by Erik Kraft (BridgeWater Books, 1998)
    —*The Edible Pyramid* by Loreen Leedy (Holiday House, Inc.; 1996)

• Give this lunch-ratings activity two thumbs-up! Ask each student to write an original lunch menu on a sheet of paper. Explain to him that for this activity, he may write a healthful menu or one that has little nutritional value. Next direct each youngster to trade his completed menu with a classmate. Then write the menu-rating scale shown below on the chalkboard. Have each student review his classmate's menu and then use the scale to rate it. Ask him to write the rating at the top of the menu. Instruct each student to return the rated menu to its owner and explain to him how he determined the rating. Also have him give the owner suggestions for making the menu more nutritious. No doubt this activity will give students food for thought!

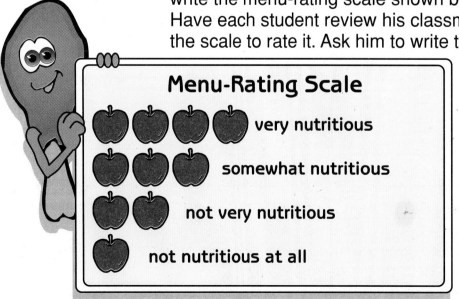

Menu-Rating Scale

very nutritious

somewhat nutritious

not very nutritious

not nutritious at all

Busy Bones

Standing up or sitting down, our bones help us get around!

Skill: Identifying parts of the human skeletal system

Estimated Lesson Time: 30 minutes

Teacher Preparation:
Duplicate page 49 for each student.

Materials:
1 copy of page 49 per student
scissors
glue

Background Information:

A skeleton is a very important part of a human body. It provides a strong frame-work for the body; protects its organs, such as the brain and heart; and helps it move. Without a skeleton, a body would be floppy and shapeless. An adult skeleton has 206 bones that vary in size and shape. Each bone has a special function.

- The **backbone**, or *spine*, links together the top and bottom parts of a skeleton and provides its primary support. It also balances the top part of a body over its hips and legs.
- The **skull** has 22 bones and protects the brain.
- The **upper arm** bone is also known as the *humerus*. Arms are the most mobile parts of a body.
- The **hand** has 27 bones. It is the most flexible part of the human skeleton.
- The **rib** bones curve around the body, forming a strong cage that guards the heart and lungs.
- The **pelvis**, a bowl-shaped bone, has two sockets into which the thighbones fit.
- The **thighbone**, or *femur,* is a person's longest bone. The length of one thigh-bone is equal to one-quarter of a person's total height.
- The **foot** bones grow faster than any other bones in the human body. They are flatter than hand bones, which helps people balance.

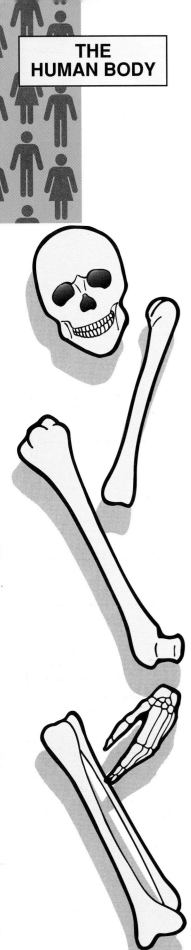

Introducing The Lesson:

Ask each student to sit up as straight as possible in her chair. Next tell her to place her hand on the center of her back and then to relax her position. Repeat these steps several times and have youngsters share their observations. Explain to each student that the bumps she felt are actually small bones that are part of her backbone, or spine—the primary support for a skeleton. Tell students that the human body has 206 bones and that this lesson will teach them about several of them.

Steps:

1. Use the Background Information on page 47 to tell students about the importance of the human skeletal system.

2. Have each student find and feel his skull; then share the related facts on page 47. Continue in a like manner with the following skeletal parts: *upper arm, hand, ribs, pelvis, thighbone,* and *foot.*

3. Give each student a copy of page 49, scissors, and glue. Review the directions with students; then have each of them complete the reproducible activity.

4. Challenge youngsters to complete the Bonus Box activity.

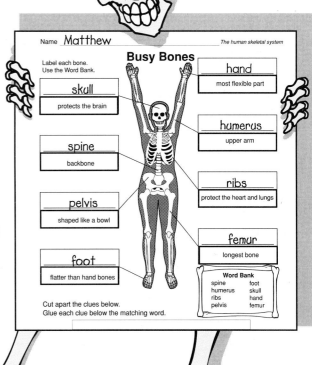

Name Matthew   The human skeletal system

Busy Bones

Label each bone.
Use the Word Bank.

| skull |
| protects the brain |

| spine |
| backbone |

| pelvis |
| shaped like a bowl |

| foot |
| flatter than hand bones |

| hand |
| most flexible part |

| humerus |
| upper arm |

| ribs |
| protect the heart and lungs |

| femur |
| longest bone |

Word Bank
spine   foot
humerus   skull
ribs   hand
pelvis   femur

Cut apart the clues below.
Glue each clue below the matching word.

Name _____

The human skeletal system

Busy Bones

Label each bone.
Use the Word Bank.

_____

_____

_____

_____

_____

_____

_____

_____

Cut apart the clues below.
Glue each clue below the matching word.

Word Bank

spine	foot
humerus	skull
ribs	hand
pelvis	femur

Bonus Box: On the back of this sheet, write two reasons our skeletons are important.

©1998 The Education Center, Inc. • Lifesaver Lessons™ • Grade 2 • TEC509 • Key p. 48

backbone	most flexible part	longest bone
protects the brain	protect the heart and lungs	flatter than hand bones
upper arm	shaped like a bowl	

49

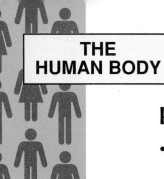
How To Extend The Lesson:

• Keep students on the move with this lesson about joints. Explain that the place where two bones meet is called a *joint*. *Ball-and-socket joints* are found in a person's shoulders and hips, and they swivel in almost any direction. *Hinge joints* are found in a person's fingers, elbows, and knees. Each of them allows movement in only one direction, like a door hinge. Have students demonstrate the movements of these two types of joints. Then show youngsters what it would be like if they didn't have joints. To begin, help a student volunteer tape a crayon to each of his fingers on one hand so that his knuckles will not bend. Next have him try to pick up a pencil or book as his classmates observe. Ask the volunteer and other students to share their observations. Repeat this exercise with other students, or complete similar experiments by taping a ruler to a student volunteer's elbow or wrist joint. If desired, provide time later in the day for the remaining students to try this exercise. Make no bones about it—this activity is a winner!

• Bone up on the skeletal system with these terrific titles!
—*The Skeleton Inside You* by Philip Balestrino (HarperCollins Publishers, Inc.; 1989)
—*Dem Bones* by Bob Barner (Chronicle Books, 1996)
—*Body Books: Bones* by Anna Sandeman (The Millbrook Press, Inc.; 1995)

• Host a "bone-a fide" bone-building snack time! Tell students that calcium-rich foods—such as milk, cheese, and spinach—help to grow strong bones. Ask each student to bring a calcium-rich snack to school on a predetermined day. As youngsters munch away on their healthful treats, share the facts below.
—Both the human neck and the giraffe neck have seven bones.
—Skeletons in laboratories are white because their bones have been lightened. The bones of a living skeleton vary from beige to pink.
—A very young person has approximately 300 bones. As he grows, some of them fuse together, so an adult skeleton has 206 bones.
—A person's muscles weigh more than his bones.
—The smallest human bone is in the ear. It is smaller than a grain of rice.

Tooth Wisdom

Smile! It's time to brush up on dental health!

Skill: Identifying good dental-health habits

Estimated Lesson Time: 45 minutes

Teacher Preparation:
1. Visually divide a sheet of bulletin-board paper into two columns. Label one column "Foods That Make My Smile Bright." Label the other column "Foods That Make My Smile A Fright."
2. Draw a tooth character with a bright smile in the left column of the labeled paper and a tooth character with a gap-toothed grin in the right column, as shown on page 52.
3. Duplicate page 53 for each student.

Materials:
1 large sheet of prepared bulletin-board paper (see page 52)
1 discarded magazine per every two students
1 copy of page 53 per student
scissors
glue

Background Information:
Good dental habits prevent most cases of tooth decay. Three major components of dental care recommended by dentists follow.
- **A healthful diet:** Eat well-balanced meals and few sugary foods to avoid cavities. Foods that are high in calcium—such as cheese, yogurt, and milk—are especially important for keeping teeth strong and healthy. Fluorides are also helpful; they help teeth resist cavity-forming acid. You can get fluorides in a variety of ways (drinking water, tablets prescribed by your dentist, toothpaste, etc.).
- **Clean teeth:** Brush your teeth after every meal and floss once a day. These practices remove food particles and plaque from teeth. Food particles attract germs, which gather on the surface of teeth and form a thin layer called plaque. If the plaque is not brushed away, it will cause tooth decay.
- **Dental checkups:** Visit your dentist at least once a year. With regular appointments, dentists can recognize and treat dental diseases before they cause serious damage.

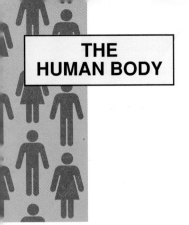

Introducing The Lesson:

Display the prepared chart (similar to the one shown below). Read the first column heading with youngsters and ask them to brainstorm nutritious foods that help keep teeth healthy. Then read the second heading with youngsters. Tell them that foods with a lot of sugar can make teeth unhealthy. Ask students to name some foods that belong in this category.

Steps:

1. Tell students that they will complete this chart as a class by adding magazine pictures to it. Divide students into pairs and give each pair a magazine and scissors.

2. Ask each youngster to cut out one picture of food from the magazine.

3. Have each student in turn show the class his picture, classify it as either a food that is good for teeth or one that is harmful, and glue it onto the chart in the appropriate column.

4. Explain to youngsters that in addition to eating nutritious foods, there are other ways to keep their teeth healthy. Share the Background Information on page 51.

5. Give each student a copy of page 53. Read the directions and Word Bank with youngsters.

6. Read each sentence with students and have each youngster complete it on his sheet. Then read the directions at the bottom of the page and have each student solve the riddle.

7. Challenge students to complete the Bonus Box activity.

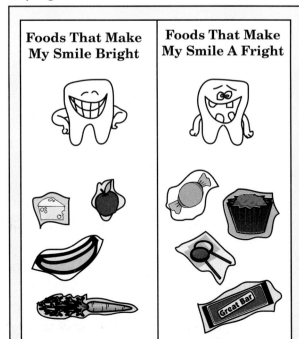

Foods That Make My Smile Bright	Foods That Make My Smile A Fright

Name _____ *Good dental-health habits*

Tooth Wisdom

Complete each sentence.
Use the Word Bank.

1. Visit your __ __ __ __ [4] __ [7] at least once a year.

2. [2] __ __ __ __ your teeth after every meal.

3. If you don't brush well, __ __ [1] __ __ [12] will form on your teeth.

4. Clean between your teeth with __ __ __ [8] __ .

5. Eat [6] __ __ __ __ __ __ [11] foods.

6. Water and toothpaste with __ __ __ __ [3] [10] __ __ help prevent cavities.

7. [9] __ __ __ keeps teeth strong.

8. __ __ [5] __ __ __ treats can cause cavities.

What do you get when you cross good dental habits with a smart student?
Write the letter from each numbered box below to find the answer!

___   ___ ___ ___ ___ ___ ___   ___ ___ ___ ___ ___ !
1   2   3   4   5   6   7   8   9   10   11   12

Bonus Box: On the back of this sheet, draw and label three foods that are good for your teeth.

(53)

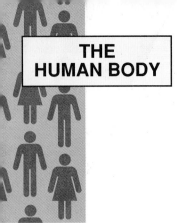

How To Extend The Lesson:

- Brush up on math and critical-thinking skills with this "tooth-errific" graphing activity! On chart paper, draw and label a graph for a question related to dental health, such as "What color is your toothbrush?" or "How many toothbrushes are in your bathroom?" Have each student respond to the question by personalizing and taping a tooth or toothbrush cutout to the graph in the appropriate location. Then analyze the results with youngsters. Now that's an idea that you can count on!

- Give students practice flossing with this fun simulation. Give each pair of students a 12-inch length of yarn. Instruct one student in each pair to hold up his hands and put them together, palm to palm. Then have him slightly spread apart his fingers to represent teeth. Direct his partner to guide his yarn between the first set of fingers and pull it up and down, "cleaning" the sides of the "teeth." Have him repeat this step with the remaining "teeth." Then ask each youngster to switch roles with his partner. Encourage each student to put his flossing skills into practice with real floss at home.

- Your young book lovers will have something to smile about with this project! Duplicate on tagboard a class supply of the bookmark below. Give each student a copy; then have her personalize her bookmark and cut it out. Review the listed titles with youngsters and encourage them to use their bookmarks as they enjoy these books. At the end of your dental-health study, give each student a tooth-shaped or gold-star sticker to place beside her favorite "toothy" title.

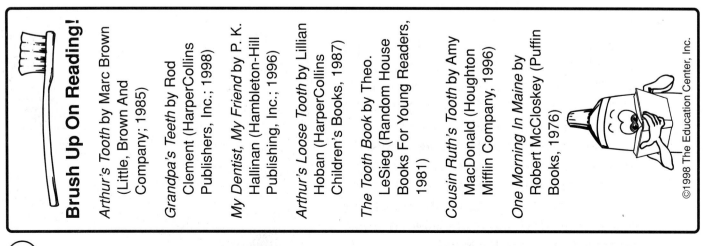

Brush Up On Reading!

Arthur's Tooth by Marc Brown (Little, Brown And Company; 1985)

Grandpa's Teeth by Rod Clement (HarperCollins Publishers, Inc.; 1998)

My Dentist, My Friend by P. K. Hallinan (Hambleton-Hill Publishing, Inc.; 1996)

Arthur's Loose Tooth by Lillian Hoban (HarperCollins Children's Books, 1987)

The Tooth Book by Theo. LeSieg (Random House Books For Young Readers, 1981)

Cousin Ruth's Tooth by Amy MacDonald (Houghton Mifflin Company, 1996)

One Morning In Maine by Robert McCloskey (Puffin Books, 1976)

©1998 The Education Center, Inc.

Planets On Parade

*Send your students into orbit with an out-of-this-world lesson
on planet order!*

Skill: Identifying planet order

Estimated Lesson Time: 25 minutes

Teacher Preparation:

1. Duplicate page 57 for each student.
2. On the chalkboard, draw the solar system illustration similar to the one shown on page 56. Exclude the planet names.
3. Make a list of the nine planets on the chalkboard.

Materials:

1 copy of page 57 per student
glue
scissors

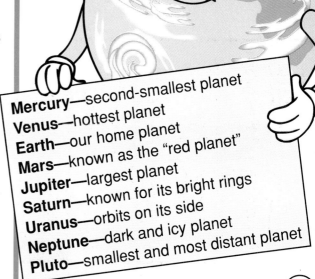

Background Information:

- All the planets move around the Sun in the same direction.
- The Sun's gravitational pull keeps the planets in a path around itself.
- Each planet spins, or *rotates,* as it revolves around the Sun. The farther a planet is from the Sun, the longer it takes to complete the orbital path around it and the longer the year. The planets' rotation periods (the time required to spin around once) range from less than ten hours for Jupiter to 243 days for Venus. Earth rotates once every 24 hours.
- The list at the right gives a short description of each planet. (Planets are listed in order going outward from the Sun.)

Mercury—second-smallest planet
Venus—hottest planet
Earth—our home planet
Mars—known as the "red planet"
Jupiter—largest planet
Saturn—known for its bright rings
Uranus—orbits on its side
Neptune—dark and icy planet
Pluto—smallest and most distant planet

Introducing The Lesson:

Tell students the word *planet* comes from a Greek word meaning *to wander.* Ask your class to guess why ancient people might have chosen that name for the planets. Lead students to realize that the planets wander by moving in paths, or *orbits,* around the Sun.

Steps:

1. Refer to the illustration on the chalkboard as you share the information from the first three items of Background Information on page 55.

2. Next tell students that the illustration shows the location of each of the nine planets from the Sun. Then point to the planet closest to the Sun, Mercury, and share its short description with students. Ask a student volunteer to find the word *Mercury* on the list (located on the chalkboard). Then have him copy the planet's name on the corresponding drawing.

3. Continue in this same manner with the remaining planets.

4. Distribute glue, scissors, and a copy of page 57 to each student. Instruct her to complete the page by cutting out and gluing each planet to its correct orbit.

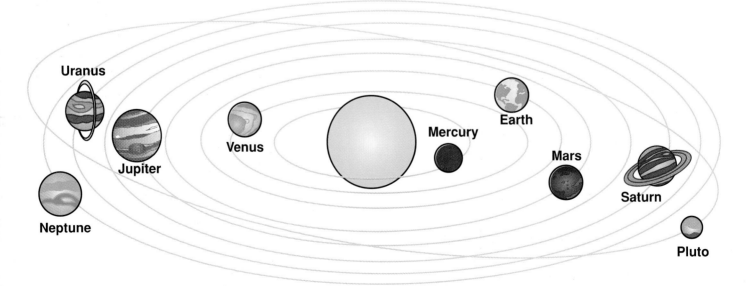

Uranus

Neptune

Jupiter

Venus

Mercury

Earth

Mars

Saturn

Pluto

Planets On Parade

Cut out the planets. Glue them in the correct order.

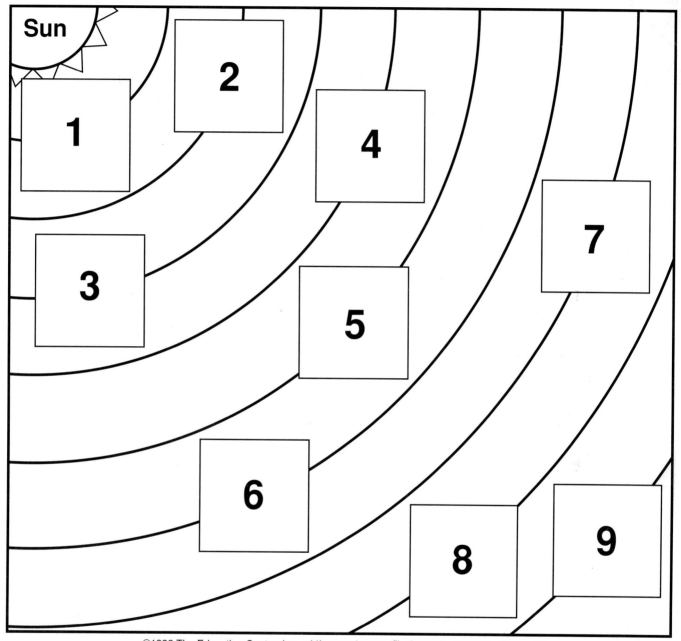

Sun

1 2 3 4 5 6 7 8 9

Pluto   Neptune   Venus   Mercury   Uranus

Earth   Jupiter   Mars   Saturn

How To Extend The Lesson:

• Display the sentence "**M**y **V**ery **E**nergetic **M**other **J**ust **S**ewed **U**s **N**ine **P**illows!" Show students that the first letter of each word corresponds with the first letter of each planet in the solar system. Also explain that the words are arranged in the planets' correct order from the Sun. After your students become familiar with the learning device, encourage them to make up other sentences using the first letter of each planet in the correct sequence. Provide time for students to share their solar sentences with the class.

• Have your students work in small groups to create an out-of this-world display. Challenge each group to use modeling clay to create a model of the solar system. Challenge students to show the planets roughly to scale. To display the planets, have each group arrange its planets in the correct order in a large shallow box.

• Use this nifty idea to display an eye-catching reproduction of the solar system on your playground. Label poster-board cutouts to represent the Sun and each of the nine planets. Also label a resealable plastic bag for each planet. Cut string lengths using the chart below, and place each length of string in its corresponding bag. On the playground, position the Sun cutout in an open area. Seat students near the Sun cutout. Then, for each planet, have student volunteers tape one end of its corresponding length of string to the Sun cutout and walk away from the Sun. When the string's end is reached, tape the corresponding planet cutout to it.

Planet	Distance From The Sun	String Length
Mercury	36 million miles	1 foot
Venus	67 million miles	approx. 2 feet
Earth	93 million miles	approx. 2.5 feet
Mars	142 million miles	approx. 4 feet
Jupiter	484 million miles	approx. 13.5 feet
Saturn	885 million miles	approx. 24.5 feet
Uranus	1,780 million miles	approx. 49.5 feet
Neptune	2,790 million miles	approx. 77.5 feet
Pluto	3,660 million miles	approx. 101.5 feet

Our Sunny Neighbor

*Get ready for a "sun-sational" lesson about our source
of heat, light, and energy.*

Skill: Recognizing the Sun's importance

Estimated Lesson Time: 30 minutes

Teacher Preparation:
Duplicate page 61 for each student.

Materials:
1 copy of page 61 per student
one 6" x 20" strip of
   bulletin-board paper
scissors
glue
crayons
colored chalk

Background Information:
Want the scoop on the Sun? Then share the following bright facts with your students:
• The Sun is a medium-sized star—a bright, big ball of burning gas.
• Although the Sun's average distance from Earth is about 93 million miles, it is closer than any other star.
• It weighs 2 billion billion billion tons (that's 2 with 27 zeros after it).
• The Sun's gravity is 28 times greater than Earth's. If you weigh 100 pounds on Earth, you'd weigh almost 1.5 tons on the Sun.
• Its surface temperature is 11,000° F. Things are hotter in the core; temperatures there reach 27,000,000° F.
• Light takes only 8 minutes and 20 seconds to zoom from the Sun to Earth. The fastest jet on Earth would take a million times that long. Some stars you see at night are so far away that their light takes 4,000 years to reach Earth.

Introducing The Lesson:

Use colored chalk to draw a picture of the Sun on the chalkboard. Ask students why they think the Sun is important to us. Accept reasonable responses; then confirm that the Sun is an important source of heat, light, and energy.

Steps:

1. Explain to students that the Sun's light and heat make life possible on Earth. Plants make their food with photosynthesis, which is dependent on the Sun. All other life is dependent on plants or plant eaters. For example, plants give us food to eat and oxygen to breathe. Tell students that they are going to help you illustrate an example of how important the Sun is to our planet.

2. To create the example shown below, draw a line to represent the ground under the drawing of the Sun. Also draw a small kernel of corn planted below the ground. Tell the class that the Sun's heat and light will help the seed to sprout. Ask a student volunteer to draw the seed sprouting (to the right of the seed drawing). Then, in turn, explain each of the following stages and have a volunteer draw the provided symbol (of the stage) on the chalkboard.
   — The Sun's heat and light help the corn plant grow (mature corn plant).
   — After the corn is harvested, it is used in many ways (a bag of corn feed).
   — Corn is used in some chicken feed (chicken).
   — Chickens provide us with eggs (a carton of eggs).
   — People sometimes eat eggs for breakfast (a plate of eggs).

3. Connect the pictures with arrows as shown below. Remind students that without the Sun, we would not be alive. There also would not be any plants, animals that eat plants, or products we get from those animals.

4. Distribute scissors, glue, crayons, paper strips, and a copy of page 61 to each student. Explain that each student will complete a diagram showing how the Sun helps our planet. To make a diagram (similar in style to the one shown), a student colors and cuts out the pictures, then cuts out the labels. Next he matches the pictures with their corresponding labels, then glues the picture-word pairs to the drawing paper to indicate how the Sun indirectly provides milk for people to drink.

MILK

| The Sun gives off heat and light. | The cow produces milk. | Grass and plants grow. |
| The child drinks the milk. | A cow eats the grass. | |

How To Extend The Lesson:

• On the next sunny day, use this experiment to show students why some things get hotter in the Sun than others. Place an ice cube in the center of a sheet of construction paper in each of the following colors: black, white, red, blue, and yellow. Then enlist students' help in timing how long it takes each ice cube to melt. Lead students to realize that light colors reflect heat, so they stay cooler, and dark colors absorb heat, so they stay warmer. For an added challenge, enlist students' help in demonstrating that shiny, smooth surfaces also reflect heat, whereas rough, dull surfaces keep heat in.

• To show your students how Earth revolves around the Sun, follow the shadows! Early in the day, use chalk to trace the shadow of a permanent fixture that is cast upon a sidewalk or paved area. Follow the changing shape throughout the day by having students visit the sight to observe the shadow's movement. If desired, retrace the shadow as it moves throughout the day and record the time by each tracing. No doubt students will be impressed with this visible account of our planet's journey around the Sun.

• Review with students how important the Sun is with this illuminating bulletin-board display. Cover a bulletin board with blue bulletin-board paper; then mount a large yellow circle in the center of the board. Give each student a small yellow construction-paper triangle. (Be sure the triangles are equilateral). On his triangle, have him write one way that we depend on the Sun. Provide time for each child to share his information with the class. Then staple the triangles to the board as shown to create the Sun's rays. To complete the display, add facial features and sunglasses on the sun and mount the title.

Our Marvelous Moon

Is it made of green cheese? Did a cow really jump over it?
Uncover the real facts about the Moon with this far-out activity!

Skill: Learning about the Moon

Estimated Lesson Time: 30 minutes

Teacher Preparation:
1. Duplicate page 65 onto tagboard for each student.
   Use an X-acto® knife to slit the dotted lines on each moon.
2. Write "Hey diddle diddle, the cat and the fiddle, the cow…"
   on the chalkboard.

Materials:
1 tagboard copy of page 65 per student
1 sheet of writing paper per student
crayons
scissors
glue
X-acto® knife

Background Information:
Share a little lunar learning with these fascinating facts about the Moon.
• The Moon is a huge rock.
• It is the Earth's nearest neighbor in space. If you could walk to the moon, it would take almost ten years to get there. A rocket trip to the Moon and back takes about six days.
• The Moon is wide enough to cover Australia.
• It is over 4 1/2 billion years old.
• The Moon weighs 81 million trillion tons (81,000,000,000,000,000,000). Earth is 80 times heavier.
• If the Moon were seen next to the Earth, it would look like a tennis ball next to a basketball.

Introducing The Lesson:

Direct students' attention to the nursery rhyme phrase on the chalkboard. Ask your students to supply the ending to the rhyme *("…jumped over the moon.")*. Inform your class that there are two images in that sentence that could not be true—a cat playing a fiddle and a cow jumping over the Moon.

Steps:

1. Explain to your class that there are several *myths,* or untrue beliefs, about the Moon. One is that the moon is made of green cheese. This myth was probably created because the *craters,* or holes, on the Moon's surface make it look like Swiss cheese. Another myth is that there is a man in the Moon. This myth probably comes from the fact that the Moon has dark markings on it that form a pattern like a face.

2. Share the Background Information on page 63 with your students. Then tell them that they will review additional information about the Moon as they create the following project.

3. Distribute crayons, glue, a pair of scissors, and a copy of page 65 to each student. To make a moon tachistoscope, a student colors his moon pattern; then he cuts out the moon and the strips. Next he cuts the moon pattern on the dotted lines, glues the three strips together where indicated, and inserts the resulting strip into the moon.

4. Have each student number a sheet of paper from 1 to 18. Then, to use the tachistoscope, each student positions the strip so he can view the first question. He reads the statement, then indicates on his paper if the statement is "true" or "false." The student continues in this manner with the remaining statements.

5. After students have responded to each question, use the answer key on page 95 to review the answers. If desired, have each student also write "T" (true) or "F" (false) beside each fact on the strip. Encourage students to share these nifty moon facts with their families.

1. The Earth has more than one moon.

2. The Moon makes and gives off its own light.

3. The sky is always black on the Moon.

4. Objects weigh less on the Moon than they do on Earth.

5. The Moon has just a few craters.

Fact Or Fiction?

8. There is no air, wind, water, or weather on the Moon.

10. There is no noise on the Moon.

11. Astronauts on the Moon must carry air to breathe.

12. The Moon travels around the Earth in a path called an orbit.

13. It takes the Moon a year to travel around the Earth once.

14. The Moon changes shape throughout the month.

15. Each Moon shape you see is called a phase.

16. Astronauts have walked on the Moon.

17. Astronauts on the Moon must wear space suits.

18. The surface of the Moon changes constantly.

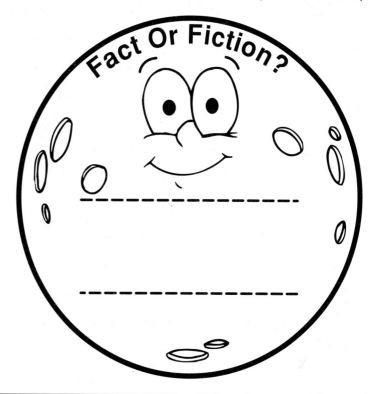

Fact Or Fiction?

1. The Earth has more than one moon.

2. The Moon makes and gives off its own light.

3. The sky is always black on the Moon.

4. Objects weigh less on the Moon than they do on Earth.

5. The Moon has just a few craters.

6. The Moon's craters were caused by spaceships.

7. Craters can be as tiny as pinholes or as large as cities.

8. There is no air, wind, water, or weather on the Moon.

9. There are many living things on the Moon.

Glue here.

10. There is no noise on the Moon.

11. Astronauts on the Moon must carry air to breathe.

12. The Moon travels around the Earth in a path called an orbit.

13. It takes the Moon a year to travel around the Earth once.

14. The Moon changes shape throughout the month.

Glue here.

15. Each Moon shape you see is called a phase.

16. Astronauts have walked on the Moon.

17. Astronauts on the Moon must wear space suits.

18. The surface of the Moon changes constantly.

How To Extend The Lesson:

New
Moon

Crescent

First
Quarter
(Half Moon)

Gibbous

Full
Moon

Gibbous

Last
Quarter
(Half Moon)

Crescent

- Demonstrate how the Moon shines with this experiment. Have students observe a reflector or a mirror in a dark room or a box so that no light can reach it. Then shine a flashlight on the object. Students will observe that the object does not create its own light; it only reflects the beam from the flashlight. This is similar to the way the Moon reflects the light of the Sun.

- Students will discover how craters are made with this activity. Fill a large container with sand and gather a variety of round objects such as tennis balls, golf balls, marbles, and Ping-Pong® balls. Ask a student to drop an object on the sand. Carefully remove the object and have students talk about what they see. Invite additional students to repeat the activity using the remaining objects. Encourage students to share ideas about the differences in the size of the craters created with each drop.

- Explain to students that some people use the Moon to predict the weather. Share the weather sayings below; then encourage students to watch the Moon and the weather to determine if these sayings are believable.
  —A full moon on Saturday means rain on Sunday.
  —Thunderstorms will happen two days after you see a new moon.
  —A pale moon means rain is coming.
  —A halo around the Moon means rain or snow.

- Turn your students on to Moon watching with this appealing activity. In advance create a construction-paper model of each Moon phase (see the illustration). Also write the name of each Moon phase on a separate index card. Code the back of each matching pair for self-checking. To begin, explain to students that although from Earth the Moon seems to change shape, it really doesn't. The appearance of the Moon depends on how much of it is lit by the Sun. Use the Moon phase models to show students each phase of the Moon. (The lighted part is what is seen from Earth.) Also explain that the whole process takes about a month. Then place the models and labels at a center. A student matches each word card to its matching Moon, then flips the pieces to check his work.

Conservation Counts!

*Show students that they can really make a difference
with this lesson focusing on conservation tips!*

Skill: Classifying conservation practices

Estimated Lesson Time: 30 minutes

Teacher Preparation:
Duplicate page 69 for each student.

Materials:
1 copy of page 69 per student
crayons

Background Information:
Share the following earth-friendly information with your students.
- *Conservation* is the management, protection, and wise use of natural resources. Natural resources include all the things that help support life, such as sunlight, water, soil, minerals, plants, and animals.
- Earth has limited supplies of many natural resources.
- Conservationists work to make sure that the environment can continue to provide for human needs.
- Eight main categories of conservation include soil, water, forest, grazing lands, wildlife, mineral, energy, and urban. (Urban includes air pollution, waste removal, and litter.)

THE EARTH

Introducing The Lesson:

Ask students to think about something they really love to eat. Then tell students to imagine that Earth's supply of this product is running out. Ask students how they would feel and what they could do to make the product last longer. Accept reasonable responses; then explain that Earth, just like their favorite foods, is something valuable and therefore worth protecting.

Steps:

1. Clarify that when you have something valuable or useful, it is called a *resource*. When you try to save a resource from being wasted, you *conserve* that resource. Explain that Earth is valuable because, in addition to being our home, it provides us with many resources. We need to conserve these items so that they will be plentiful in the future.

2. Share the Background Information on page 67. Ask students to name reasons why it is important to conserve each of the eight resources mentioned in the Background Information. (See the list below for examples.)

3. Distribute crayons and a copy of page 69 to each student. Explain that this activity reviews only three types of conservation: water, energy, and forest (which includes paper). Read aloud the directions and provide time for students to complete the activity.

4. Challenge students to complete the Bonus Box activity.

- **Soil conservation** is essential for the growth of plants, which in turn provide food for animals and human beings.
- **Water conservation** is important because water is used for bathing, cooking, drinking, cleaning, transportation, recreation, irrigating croplands, producing electric power, and manufacturing many products.
- **Forest conservation** is needed because forests serve as sources of timber, homes for wildlife, watersheds, and recreation areas.
- **Conservation of grazing lands** is essential because these areas support a wide variety of wildlife.
- **Wildlife conservation** is important because wild animals and plants are essential parts of nature. Wildlife is also important in scientific research.
- **Mineral conservation** is needed because industries use minerals—such as copper, gold, iron, lead, and salt—to manufacture countless products.
- **Energy conservation** is important because energy is needed in transportation and recreation, for many appliances, and for industries to operate.
- **Urban conservation** is essential to control air pollution, waste, litter, and overcrowding in cities.

Classifying conservation practices

Conservation Counts!

Use the color code to show which resource is being conserved.

Color Code: blue—water   green—forest   yellow—energy

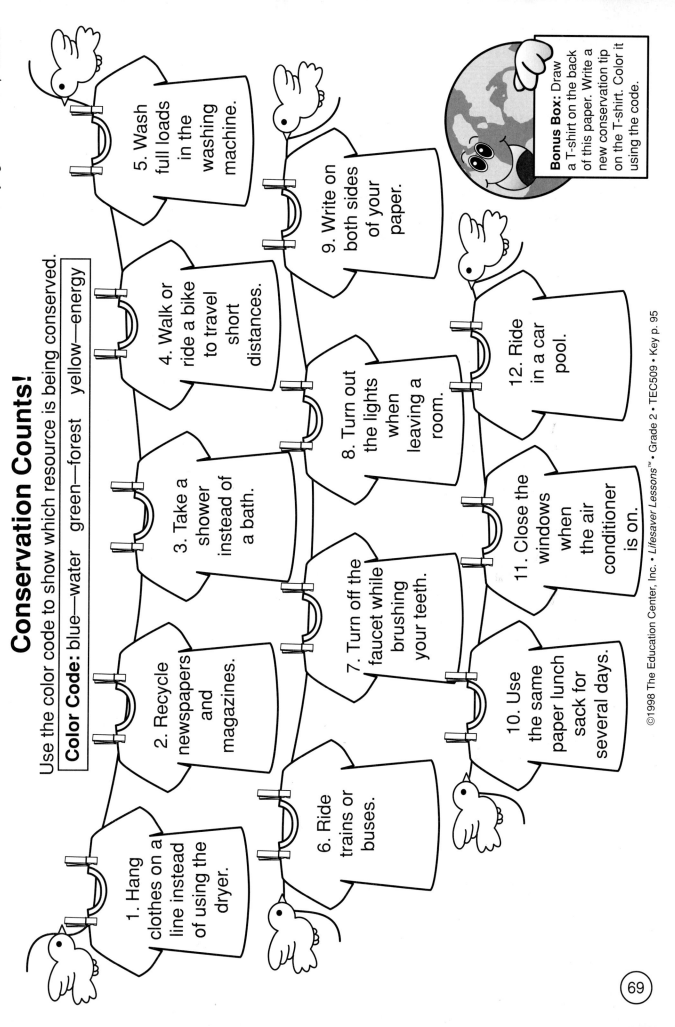

1. Hang clothes on a line instead of using the dryer.

2. Recycle newspapers and magazines.

3. Take a shower instead of a bath.

4. Walk or ride a bike to travel short distances.

5. Wash full loads in the washing machine.

6. Ride trains or buses.

7. Turn off the faucet while brushing your teeth.

8. Turn out the lights when leaving a room.

9. Write on both sides of your paper.

10. Use the same paper lunch sack for several days.

11. Close the windows when the air conditioner is on.

12. Ride in a car pool.

Bonus Box: Draw a T-shirt on the back of this paper. Write a new conservation tip on the T-shirt. Color it using the code.

How To Extend The Lesson:

• Reinforce good conservation practices with this small-group activity. Divide students into four groups and designate a recorder in each one. Give each recorder a colorful marker and a sheet of chart paper that you've labeled with one of the following categories: *water, energy, paper,* and *minerals.* Then, for three or four minutes, have each group brainstorm ways to conserve its assigned resource. Next have each group rotate to a different chart along a predetermined route. Instruct each group to read the conservation practices listed on the new sheet and to brainstorm additional ways for the group's recorder to add to the list. Repeat the activity as described until every group has had the opportunity to brainstorm and list conservation practices for each of the four categories. Then collect the charts, post them for easy viewing, and discuss the ideas listed on each chart.

• This homework task will get the whole family thinking about conservation. Instruct each student to interview her family members to see what steps they take to conserve resources. Have her write the answers on a sheet of paper. Provide time during the next school day for students to share their findings. If desired, have your class use the results to make a conservation newsletter to send home.

• Spread the news that conservation counts with this nifty display! Cut out a colorful construction-paper T-shirt for each student. Then have each student use a marker to write a conservation tip on his cutout. To display the completed projects, suspend two lengths of yarn across a bulletin board and attach the T-shirts with clothespins. For a finishing touch, add the title "We Have Conservation To A 'T'!"

A Rootin'-Tootin' Region Roundup

Your buckaroos are sure to hoot and holler as they learn about the earth's environments piece by piece!

Skill: Identifying different environments

Estimated Lesson Time: 30 minutes

Teacher Preparation:
Duplicate page 73 onto white
construction paper for each student.

Materials:
1 construction-paper copy of page 73 per
student
one 9" x 12" sheet of colored construction paper
per student
world map
scissors
glue

Background Information:

- **Deserts** are regions in the world where there is very little rainfall. They are extremely dry and can be found in very cold or very warm climates. Some deserts are vast expanses of sand; others are rocky or covered with thin scrub.
- **Oceans and seas** are the largest natural habitat. Oceans, which cover about 70 percent of the earth's surface, have a dramatic landscape—deep valleys, reefs, volcanoes, and mountains taller than any on land.
- **Polar regions**, areas around Antarctica and the Arctic, have a very cold and dry climate. Winters can last for as long as nine months, with subzero temperatures and total darkness. During the summer months, when there is daylight for nearly 24 hours a day, the temperature rises above freezing and some ice melts. The earth below the surface stays frozen throughout the year.
- **Grasslands** are usually flat and have rich soil that can produce good grasses but few trees (because there is not enough rain or because the ground is too dry and sandy). Different countries have different names for their grasslands, such as *savannas* in East Africa and *prairies* in North America.
- **Mountains** are landforms that stand much higher than their surroundings. They contain a wide variety of environments, from dense forest to bare, rocky ground. This variety is because weather conditions change all the way up a mountain.
- **Forests** vary throughout the world. The kind of forest in an area depends on the area's climate and rainfall. Four major types of forests are tropical rain forests, temperate rain forests, coniferous forests, and deciduous forests.

Introducing The Lesson:

Ask students to describe a variety of areas such as their hometown, vacation spots, and their relatives' hometowns. Encourage students to describe the weather conditions and land in these areas. Then inform your class that these are called *regions* or *environments.* Explain that these areas are classified by the surrounding conditions.

Steps:

1. Tell students that a region or an environment includes all the living and nonliving things in a particular area, such as the amount of water, the amount of sunlight, the temperature, and the condition of the soil.

2. To convey that there are many different kinds of environments on the earth, share the Background Information on page 71. Then challenge students to find an example of each environment on a world map. (See the information below for examples.)

3. Distribute scissors, glue, a sheet of colored construction paper, and a copy of page 73 to each student. Have each student fold her construction paper in half lengthwise and then in thirds to create six equal sections. Next have her unfold her paper.

4. Have each student cut out the puzzle pieces and then to read the clues to find the matching pairs. Finally, have her glue each matching pair to a separate section on her sheet of construction paper.

5. After each student completes the activity, have her draw a star beside the puzzle-piece pair that best describes the region where she lives.

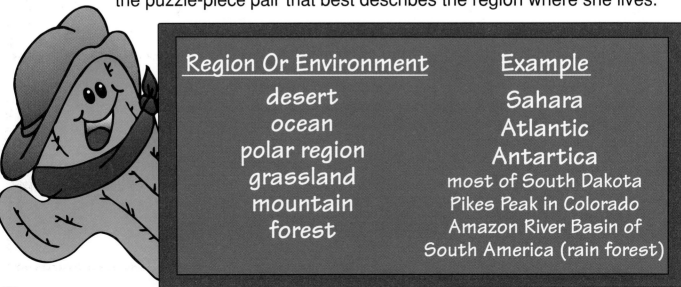

Region Or Environment	Example
desert	Sahara
ocean	Atlantic
polar region	Antartica
grassland	most of South Dakota
mountain	Pikes Peak in Colorado
forest	Amazon River Basin of South America (rain forest)

oceans and seas

cold lands often frozen under the surface

flat areas with good grasses and few trees

landforms that stand much higher than their surroundings

forests

deserts

vary depending on the area's climate and rainfall

largest natural habitat

polar regions

grasslands

mountains

very dry; sandy, rocky, or covered with thin scrub

How To Extend The Lesson:

• Take students on a trip through the different regions with this first-class writing activity. Ask each student to choose the region she would most like to visit. Pair the youngsters according to their preferences; then challenge each twosome to research its region. Next give each child a large, blank index card. A student illustrates one side of the card with a scene that represents the chosen region. On the back of her card–in the upper left-hand corner—she writes a brief, informative caption about the illustration. Next she writes a message (as if she were in the region) and addresses her card to her family. To complete the project, she draws a stamp in the upper right-hand corner of the card. Send these one-of-a-kind cards home by special student delivery.

• Take a more in-depth look at the earth's environments with *Our Natural Homes: Exploring Terrestrial Biomes Of North And South America* by Sneed B. Collard (Charlesbridge Publishing, Inc.; 1996). This informative book defines the earth's land ecosystems through the characteristic plants and animals found in each.

• For a fun cooperative-group activity, have students work together to create unique posters that advertise the various regions of the earth. Assign each of six student groups a different region. Instruct each group to design a colorful poster that advertises the region and persuades others to want to live in this area. If desired, encourage each group to use reference materials to determine the animals, plants, and people that live in the region, and to discover the occupations, homes, forms of entertainment, and natural resources found there. Provide the groups with white poster board, construction paper, markers, and other poster-making supplies. Set aside time for each group to present its completed poster; then display the eye-catching projects in the hallway for others to view.

Dive into the largest habitat:

The Ocean!

The ocean just might be the place for you if you enjoy
• swimming
• salt water
• staying wet
• beautiful underground landscapes
• mingling with fish
• collecting shells

☆ Remember to bring your own air tank!

Delectable Desserts

*Cook up a little classification practice
with this appetizing lesson about attributes.*

Skill: Classifying solids by attributes

Estimated Lesson Time: 30 minutes

Teacher Preparation:
1. Duplicate page 77 for each student.
2. Duplicate enough dessert patterns from the bottom of page 77 for each student to have one pattern.

Materials:
1 copy of page 77 per student
1 dessert pattern from page 77 per student
crayons
scissors
glue
tape

Background Information:
- *Matter* has weight and takes up space. It can be touched or held. All objects consist of matter and occupy space.
- Matter can be described by naming its properties. Some properties of matter are size, shape, texture, color, and temperature.
- Matter can exist in three states: *solid, liquid,* or *gas.*
  — A solid has a distinct shape and resists change in shape.
  — A liquid has no shape of its own and takes the shape of the container that holds it.
  — A gas has no definite shape and can expand indefinitely. Gases are not usually visible.

Introducing The Lesson:

On the chalkboard, draw a large triangle, circle, and square. Explain that we often sort things using *attributes,* or special features that an object has. Then tell students that they will use the figures on the chalkboard to sort some bakery items.

Steps:

1. Distribute crayons, scissors, and a copy of one of the dessert patterns (page 77) to each student. Provide time for each student to color his pattern.

2. Ask one student at a time to come to the chalkboard and tape his dessert pattern in the figure that most resembles his dessert. Inform students that they just used the attribute of shape to sort objects.

3. Ask students to name other ways they could sort their dessert patterns. List their responses on the chalkboard. If desired, have students retrieve their dessert patterns and play another round of sorting using a different attribute.

4. Distribute glue and a copy of page 77 to each student. Have each student color and cut out his patterns. Announce a way for students to sort their desserts onto the bakery counters, such as square or not square. (See the list on this page for additional ideas.) Quickly verify students' papers; then ask them to clear their bakery counters. Repeat the activity for a desired number of times. Then ask each student to sort his dessert patterns into two categories. Finally, have him write his sorting rules on the lines and glue the dessert patterns to the corresponding bakery counters.

5. Challenge students to complete the Bonus Box activity.

Different Ways To Classify Desserts

circle / not a circle
square / not a square
triangle / not a triangle
chocolate / not chocolate
hard (crunchy) / soft
topping / no topping
fruit / no fruit

Name _____

Delectable Desserts

Color and cut out the bakery treats.
Follow your teacher's directions.

Desserts For Sale!

category: _____

Desserts For Sale!

category: _____

Bonus Box: On the back of this paper, list ways you could sort candy bars.

candy apple

frosted brownie

pie slice

turnover

cake slice

ice-cream cone

cookie

donut

77

How To Extend The Lesson:

• Introduce another tasty classification activity by having each student fill a small, resealable plastic bag with cereal pieces from home. Arrange the bags for easy viewing, and then have your students suggest ways of classifying the cereal pieces. List the attributes given in response; then mix the cereal pieces and distribute a cupful to each student. Conclude the activity by inviting students to munch on their cereal pieces!

• Sharpen your students' creative-thinking skills with an exercise in comparing and contrasting. Display two solids for the class to observe. Challenge each student to think of two ways that the objects are alike and two ways that they are different. For an added incentive, use objects that your students have brought from home.

• Shape up your youngsters' classification skills with this nifty idea. Cut out large shapes from bulletin-board paper and place them on the classroom floor. Divide students into as many groups as there are shapes, then assign each group a shape. At your signal, have each group search the classroom for solids that are the same shape as its designated shape. When a student finds a solid with a matching shape, she places it on the large paper shape. After a predetermined amount of time, gather students around the paper shapes to share the solids they found.

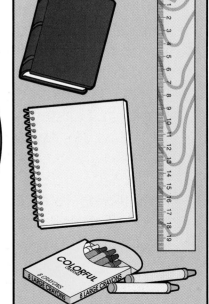

Classifying solids by attributes

What's The Source?

Work a little science magic with this lesson on the sources of heat, light, and sound. It's as fun as pulling a rabbit out of a hat!

Skill: Classifying sources of heat, light, and sound

Estimated Lesson Time: 30 minutes

Teacher Preparation:
1. Duplicate page 81 for each student.
2. On the chalkboard, draw and label a picture of each of the following items: a lightbulb, a microwave, and a drum.

Materials:
1 copy of page 81 per student

Background Information:
Heat, light, and sound are just a few of the many kinds of energy.
- Anything that gives off heat is a source of heat. There are two main sources of heat: *natural* and *man-made.* Natural sources include sunshine, volcanoes, hot springs, and lightning. Man-made sources include heat caused by friction (striking a match, running a car engine) and heat harnessed from the flow of electrons (almost all electrical appliances).
- Light sources can be classified as *natural* or *artificial.* Natural light comes from sources that cannot be controlled, such as the Sun and the stars. Artificial light comes from sources that can be controlled, such as candles and flashlights.
- Every sound is produced by the vibrations of an object. Some ways sounds may be classified are loud or soft, high or low, noise or music, sustained sounds or short sounds.

Classifying sources of heat, light, and sound (79)

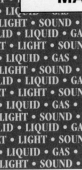

Introducing The Lesson:

Instruct students to imagine each of the following scenarios. Then ask them to describe each one.
• They are standing near a heater.
• They are looking at a lamp turned on.
• They are listening to a band play music.
Tell students that in each scenario, they experienced a type of energy—heat, light, or sound. Challenge students to match each type of energy with the corresponding scenario.

Steps:

1. Share the Background Information on page 79 with students.

2. Ask students to name sources of each type of energy: heat, light, and sound. Write their responses on the chalkboard. (See the examples below as needed.)

3. Distribute a copy of page 81 to each student. Read the directions and the words in the Word Bank with students; then provide time for students to complete the reproducible.

4. Challenge students to complete the Bonus Box activity.

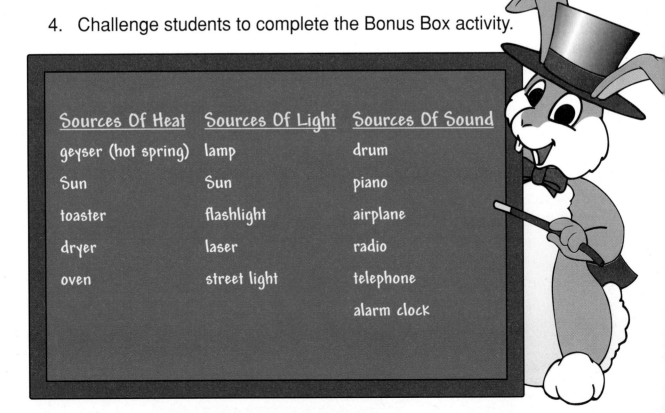

Sources Of Heat	Sources Of Light	Sources Of Sound
geyser (hot spring)	lamp	drum
Sun	Sun	piano
toaster	flashlight	airplane
dryer	laser	radio
oven	street light	telephone
		alarm clock

Name_____  *Classifying energy sources*

What's The Source?

Read the energy sources in the Word Bank.
Write each word in the correct column to show
  the type of energy for which it is a source.
Some words may fit in more than one column.

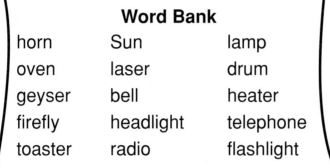

Word Bank

horn	Sun	lamp
oven	laser	drum
geyser	bell	heater
firefly	headlight	telephone
toaster	radio	flashlight

Heat	Light	Sound

Bonus Box: On the back of this paper, write one more energy source for each type of energy: heat, light, and sound.

81

How To Extend The Lesson:

- Explain to students that every sound is produced by the vibrations of an object. When an object vibrates, the object causes the molecules in the air to start vibrating. The *vibrations* (or sound waves) move outward in all directions from the object. The vibrations enter your ears, and your ears convert them to nerve impulses. The nerve impulses are then relayed to the brain, where they are interpreted as sounds. After presenting this information, share *Science Magic With Sound* by Chris Oxlade (Barron's Educational Series, Inc.; 1994). Students are sure to enjoy trying the entertaining magic tricks that use sound as the trickster. Each trick includes directions for preparing and performing the trick as well as a scientific explanation.

- Remind students that there are two main sources of heat: natural and man-made. Explain that both sources of heat are important to man, for without harnessed heat, we would not have the convenience of modern appliances. Without natural heat, we would really be in trouble—we depend on the Sun to keep our planet warm enough to live on! After sharing this information, challenge students to think about the many types of heat they use each day. Assign each student a room of a house and have him list the different types of heat found in that room. Enlist students' help in compiling the findings onto a chart labeled "Heat In Our Homes."

- Review with students the two ways light sources can be classified—as natural or artificial. Then have each student write a letter to his parents explaining the importance of light. Encourage students to also name examples of both types of light sources.

- Present each student with a personalized copy of the award shown.

_____ is a *source* of great science knowledge!

Simple-Machine Match

*Gear up students' classification skills with this
machine matching game!*

Skill: Classifying simple machines

Estimated Lesson Time: 45 minutes

Teacher Preparation:
1. Duplicate page 85 onto tagboard for each student.
2. Gather items to demonstrate each simple machine
   listed in the Background Information. (See Step 1
   on page 84.)

Materials:
1 tagboard copy of page 85 per student
scissors
materials used to demonstrate each of the six types
   of simple machines

Background Information:
There are six types of simple machines that help people work. All machines are
based on one or more of these simple machines.

- An **inclined plane** helps move
  an object upward with less
  effort than it would take to lift
  it directly. The longer the
  slope, the smaller the effort
  required. One type of inclined
  plane is a ramp.

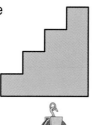

- A **pulley** is a grooved wheel
  with a rope or cable around it.
  It moves things up, down, or
  across.

- A **wheel and an axle** work together
  to disperse force. A wheel can move
  a great distance with little effort.
- A **wedge** is an object with at least
  one slanting side that ends in a
  sharp edge. It cuts or splits an
  object apart.
- A **screw** is an inclined plane
  wrapped around in a spiral. It
  holds things together or lifts.
- A **lever** helps lift a load with less
  effort. The lever is positioned on a
  pivot called a fulcrum. Seesaws
  and crowbars are levers.

Introducing The Lesson:

Tell students that machines make work easier. Explain that a machine does not have to be a complicated contraption with many parts powered by electricity. Actually, all complex machines are based in some way on six types of simple machines.

Steps:

1. Use the following objects (or similar ones) and the Background Information on page 83 to explain and demonstrate how each type of simple machine works.
   —toy car (wheel and axle)
   —ramp and toy car (inclined plane)
   —balance scale (lever)
   —window blinds (pulley)
   —plastic knife (wedge)
   —jar lid (screw)

2. Take students on a walk around the school in search of simple machines. Back in the classroom, write a student-generated list of simple machines they saw.

3. Next give students additional practice classifying simple machines with this Concentration-type game. Have each student cut out a copy of the cards on page 85. Pair students and have each twosome combine its cards, then shuffle them and place them facedown. In turn each student flips over two cards, trying to match a simple-machine name with a corresponding picture. If a match is made, the student keeps the cards and takes another turn. If the cards do not match, the student returns them to their positions, facedown, and her partner takes a turn. Play continues until all cards have been matched. The student with the most cards wins!

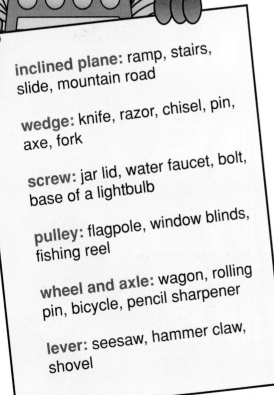

inclined plane: ramp, stairs, slide, mountain road

wedge: knife, razor, chisel, pin, axe, fork

screw: jar lid, water faucet, bolt, base of a lightbulb

pulley: flagpole, window blinds, fishing reel

wheel and axle: wagon, rolling pin, bicycle, pencil sharpener

lever: seesaw, hammer claw, shovel

inclined plane	pulley	pulley
wedge	wedge	screw
lever	lever	wheel and axle

How To Extend The Lesson:

- Try this activity to demonstrate how common simple machines are in our world. Place students in small groups. In a designated amount of time, challenge each group to find and cut out as many magazine pictures as possible of each type of simple machine. While students are working, label a sheet of poster board for each simple machine. At the end of the designated time, have each group sort its findings by type of simple machine, then glue the pictures onto the corresponding poster. Display the completed posters on a classroom wall for everyone to see!

- Ask each student to bring a toy to school. Display the toys on a table. Then, for each toy, challenge students to identify any simple machines within it.

- Sharpen students' critical-thinking skills with this activity. Write simple-machine word problems (similar to the ones shown below) on separate paper cards. Program the back of each card for self-checking; then laminate the cards and store them in a decorated container at a center. A student selects a card, answers the question, and flips the card to check her work. She continues in this manner until she answers each simple-machine question.

Leigh wants to move a large rock. What simple machines should she use?

Terrance is putting a lid on a jar. What simple machine is he using?

Living Or Nonliving?

Students' classification skills come to life with this unique game of tic-tac-toe!

Skill: Classifying living and nonliving things

Estimated Lesson Time: 30 minutes

Teacher Preparation:
1. Duplicate page 89 for each student.
2. Duplicate the patterns on page 90 for each student.

Materials:
1 copy of page 89 per student
1 copy of the patterns on page 90 per student
1 craft stick per student
scissors
glue

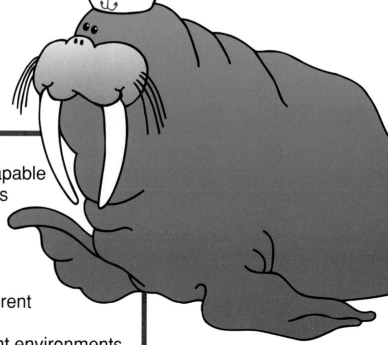

Background Information:
- We classify a thing as *living* if it is capable of certain activities. Most living things
  —grow and change
  —need air, water, and food
  —respond to their surroundings
  —reproduce more of their own kind
- There are more than ten million different species of living things on Earth.
- Living things can be found in different environments.
- All living things are made up of cells.

Introducing The Lesson:

Ask students to look around the classroom and name objects that they see. Write students' responses on the chalkboard in two lists, one for the living objects and one for the nonliving objects. (Do not reveal this method of classification.) After generating the lists, ask your students if they can determine why the objects are grouped in this manner. Confirm that the objects in one group are all living things and that the objects in the other group are nonliving.

Steps:

1. Ask students to determine the differences between the two categories. Then share the Background Information on page 87.

2. Inform students that they are going to play a game in which they have to classify living and nonliving things. To play the game, each student will need an answer wand. Have each student cut out a copy of the patterns on page 90 and then glue a craft stick between them as shown.

3. To play the game, announce the name of an object. Instruct students to display the correct side of the wand towards you to indicate if the object is living or nonliving. Repeat the activity until students can readily classify living and nonliving things.

4. Next tell students they will continue classifying living and nonliving things by playing a unique game of tic-tac-toe. Explain that one reason the game is unique is that each student plays the game by himself. Distribute a copy of page 89 to each student; then read the directions aloud. Tell students to follow the directions to complete all four grids.

5. Challenge students to complete the Bonus Box activity.

Name_____

Classifying living and nonliving things

Living Or Nonliving?

Look at each picture.
Write **N** if it shows something nonliving.
Write **L** if it shows something living.
Draw a line to show three of these letters in a row.

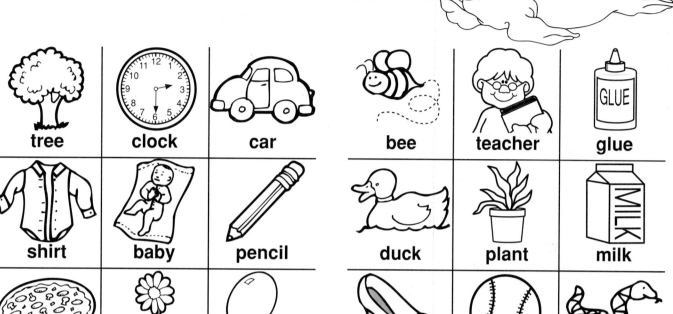

tree	clock	car	bee	teacher	glue
shirt	baby	pencil	duck	plant	milk
pizza	flower	balloon	shoe	ball	snake

dog	bus	turtle	sun	doctor	spoon
fish	house	rocket	chair	box	candle
pig	grass	cake	cat	flag	butterfly

Bonus Box: On the back of this sheet, list three ways living and nonliving things are different.

©1998 The Education Center, Inc. • Lifesaver Lessons™ • Grade 2 • TEC509 • Key p. 95

89

How To Extend The Lesson:

- Take your students on a mini field trip outside to observe living and nonliving things. Challenge each student to list on paper five living and five nonliving things. Back in the classroom, place students in small groups and challenge them to compare the items on their lists.

- Reinforce classification skills with an activity for sorting nonliving items. Ask each student to bring two or three nonliving objects from home. Place students into small groups and challenge them to sort their objects into categories, such as by shape, color, size, or function. Ask each group to explain its reasons for sorting the objects as it did.

- Have your students create posters featuring living and nonliving things. To begin, divide students into small groups and assign each group a location, such as school, a pond, or a park. Also give each group a sheet of poster board, crayons, scissors, glue, and construction paper. Have each group create a mural of its designated location; the mural should include a variety of living and nonliving things that could be found there. After the murals are complete, post them on a classroom wall. Then have students take turns labeling the items as either "living" or "nonliving."

Patterns

Living   Nonliving

All-Star Science Review

Students' science skills shine bright with this star-studded review activity.

Skill: Reviewing science concepts

Estimated Lesson Time: 25 minutes

Teacher Preparation:
Duplicate page 93 for each student.

Materials:
1 copy of page 93 per student
crayons

Teacher Reference:
Ways to use this review:
- Have students complete the review on page 93 to prepare for a test on a particular topic.
- During the last few weeks of school, review the major science topics covered during the year. Each week select a prior subject of study for your students to use as the topic in completing the reproducible. It will be a good way to assess which science concepts your students have retained.

Introducing The Lesson:

Inform students that they are going to be science stars as they evaluate the information they have learned about the current topic of study. Use the list of questions below to initiate the review. Or, if desired, have students brainstorm facts and concepts learned about the topic while you record their responses on the chalkboard.

Steps:

1. Distribute a copy of page 93 to each student.

2. Review the instructions for completing the page.

QUESTIONS TO INITIATE A SCIENCE REVIEW:

- What do you think was the most important idea in the study?
- What did you find interesting about the topic?
- Was there anything hard to understand in the study?
- Why do you think it is important to study this topic?
- What could you share about this topic with your family?

All-Star Science Review

by _____

Topic of study: _____

The most interesting fact I learned: _____

_____

Five more fun facts:

1. _____

_____

2. _____

_____

3. _____

_____

4. _____

_____

5. _____

_____

I give this science topic ☆ ☆ ☆ ☆ ☆

(Color 1, 2, 3, 4, or 5 stars. 5 stars = best.)

How To Extend The Lesson:

- Pair students and have each twosome brainstorm five facts about the designated science topic. Instruct pairs to write and illustrate each fact on a sheet of drawing paper. Then have each pair staple the pages between two construction-paper covers. Provide time for each pair to share its booklet with the class.

- Try this whole-group game for a fun science review! Have each student write a question about the current science topic on one side of an index card. Then ask him to write the answer to the question and his name on the other side of the card. Collect the completed cards and divide the students into two teams. Before beginning, remind students that they cannot answer their own questions. To play the game, read a question and call on a student volunteer from one of the teams to answer the question. If he answers correctly, award his team one point. If he answers incorrectly, call on a student volunteer from the other group to answer. Award one point to his team for a correct answer. If both teams answer incorrectly, have the student who wrote the question give the answer (no points awarded). Continue alternating between teams until all the questions have been asked. The team with the most points wins!

- Reward each student with a personalized copy of the award below for her super science efforts.

Award

_____ **is an**
(student's name)

ALL-STAR
science
student!

_____
(teacher's name)

Answer Keys

Page 21
1. pistil
2. petals
3. stamens
4. stigma
5. anther
6. pollen

Bonus Box: Accept all reasonable responses.

Page 25
1. shade
2. fruits
3. roots
4. homes
5. soap
6. yards

Bonus Box: Accept all reasonable responses.

Page 29
1. mountain goat
2. camel
3. polar bear
4. elephant
5. chimpanzee
6. owl
7. dolphin

Page 33
fur: cat, giraffe, dog, bear, fox, mouse
feathers: owl, duck, parrot, chicken
scales: snake, turtle, crocodile
1. fur
2. 9
3. 7
4. mammals
5. birds
6. reptiles

Page 41
1. apatosaurus
2. ammosaurus
3. allosaurus
4. tyrannosaurus
5. stegosaurus
6. ankylosaurus
7. triceratops
8. brachiosaurus

Page 53
1. dentist
2. brush
3. plaque
4. floss
5. healthful
6. fluoride
7. milk
8. sugary

A bright smile!

Page 57
1. Mercury
2. Venus
3. Earth
4. Mars
5. Jupiter
6. Saturn
7. Uranus
8. Neptune
9. Pluto

Page 69
1. yellow
2. green
3. blue
4. yellow
5. blue
6. yellow
7. blue
8. yellow
9. green
10. green
11. yellow
12. yellow

Page 61

The Sun gives off heat and light. | Grass and plants grow. | A cow eats the grass. | The cow produces milk. | The child drinks the milk.

Page 65
1. False—Earth only has one moon. There are other planets that have multiple moons.
2. False—Light from the Sun bounces off the Moon.
3. True—There is no atmosphere to scatter the light to see the colors in it.
4. True—The force of gravity on the Moon's surface is six times weaker than that on the surface of Earth.
5. False—You can see more than 30,000 craters from Earth.
6. False—They were caused by meteorites hitting the Moon's surface.
7. True—There are many sizes of craters on the Moon.
8. True—The Moon has no atmosphere.
9. False—There is no air or water, and the temperature is not suitable for living things.
10. True—There is no air for sound to travel through.
11. True—There is no atmosphere, which means there is no oxygen to breathe.
12. True—The path is oval shaped.
13. False—It takes almost one month.
14. False—As it moves around Earth, you see only the parts of the Moon that are lit by the Sun.
15. True—The phases follow the same pattern every four weeks.
16. True—In 1969, the Moon was the first object in space to be visited by humans.
17. True—The surface of the Moon gets much hotter and colder than any place on Earth.
18. False—Because there is no wind or rain on the Moon, its surface has changed little over billions of years.

Page 81
Heat: oven, geyser, toaster, heater, Sun
Light: firefly, laser, headlight, lamp, flashlight, Sun
Sound: horn, bell, radio, drum, telephone

Page 89
Three in a row:
car, pencil, balloon (nonliving)
bee, plant, snake (living)
dog, fish, pig (living)
chair, box, candle (nonliving)

Grade 2 Science Management Checklist

SKILLS	PAGES	DATE(S) USED	COMMENTS
WEATHER			
Types Of Weather	3		
Seasonal Attributes	7		
Thermometers	11		
PLANTS			
Life Cycle Of A Pumpkin	15		
Parts Of A Flower	19		
Trees As Valuable Resources	23		
ANIMALS			
Animal Habitats	27		
Classifying Animals	31		
Insects	35		
Dinosaurs	39		
THE HUMAN BODY			
Nutrition	43		
Bones	47		
Dental Health	51		
THE SOLAR SYSTEM			
The Planets	55		
The Sun	59		
The Moon	63		
THE EARTH			
Conservation	67		
Environments	71		
MATTER			
Classifying Solids	75		
Heat, Light, And Sound	79		
SIMPLE MACHINES			
Simple Machines	83		
BASIC SCIENCE SKILLS			
Living And Nonliving Things	87		
Science Review	91		